Beginning Azure Static Web Apps

Building and Deploying Dynamic Web Applications with Blazor

Stacy Cashmore

Apress®

Beginning Azure Static Web Apps: Building and Deploying Dynamic Web Applications with Blazor

Stacy Cashmore
Amsterdam, The Netherlands

ISBN-13 (pbk): 978-1-4842-8145-1   ISBN-13 (electronic): 978-1-4842-8146-8
https://doi.org/10.1007/978-1-4842-8146-8

Managing Director, Apress Media LLC: Welmoed Spahr
Acquisitions Editor: Smriti Srivastava
Development Editor: Laura Berendson
Coordinating Editor: Shrikant Vishwakarma

Cover designed by eStudioCalamar

Cover image designed by Pexels

Distributed to the book trade worldwide by Springer Science+Business Media LLC, 1 New York Plaza, Suite 4600, New York, NY 10004. Phone 1-800-SPRINGER, fax (201) 348-4505, email orders-ny@springer-sbm. com, or visit www.springeronline.com. Apress Media, LLC is a California LLC and the sole member (owner) is Springer Science + Business Media Finance Inc (SSBM Finance Inc). SSBM Finance Inc is a **Delaware** corporation.

For information on translations, please e-mail booktranslations@springernature.com; for reprint, paperback, or audio rights, please e-mail bookpermissions@springernature.com, or visit http://www.apress. com/rights-permissions.

Apress titles may be purchased in bulk for academic, corporate, or promotional use. eBook versions and licenses are also available for most titles. For more information, reference our Print and eBook Bulk Sales web page at http://www.apress.com/bulk-sales.

Any source code or other supplementary material referenced by the author in this book is available to readers on GitHub via the book's product page, located at https://link.springer.com/book/10.1007/ 978-1-4842-8145-1.

Printed on acid-free paper

Dedication

To Dad, one of the last things that you said to me was that if I put my mind to do something, you had no doubt it would be done. I said that I didn't believe it. Well... I've somehow managed to write this book and wish that you were here to see it. Miss you.

To my partner and child, I know that you want to remain anonymous, but I couldn't not dedicate this book to you as well. Thanks for putting up with me. Love you both!

Table of Contents

About the Author

Speaker, author, and software developer, **Stacy Cashmore** has been developing solutions since the mid-1990s in various companies and industries ranging from facilitating contract jobbing to allowing consumers to close a mortgage without the help of a financial adviser – with lots in between.

She has a passion for sharing knowledge: using story telling for sharing her experiences to help teams grow in the ways that they develop software and work together and performing live coding demonstrations to inspire others to try new technologies.

For her effort in the community, Stacy has been awarded the Microsoft MVP for Developer Technologies since 2020.

About the Technical Reviewers

Marc Duiker is a Senior Developer Advocate at Ably with a strong focus on event-driven architectures in the Azure cloud. He loves helping developers to achieve more every day.

You might have seen Marc at a developer meetup or conference since he's a regular speaker in the area of Azure cloud and serverless technologies. He started Azure Functions University, a free and open source learning curriculum on GitHub, where everyone can learn about Azure Functions at their own pace. In 2019, 2020, and 2021, Marc received the Microsoft Azure MVP award for his community contributions.

In his spare time, Marc likes to give attention to the creative part of his brain. He likes to create pixel art (check out VSCode Pets), code visuals and music, and an occasional retro game.

Jimmy Engström has been developing ever since he was seven years old and got his first computer. He loves to be on the cutting edge of technology, trying new things. When he got wind of Blazor, he immediately realized the potential and adopted it already when it was in beta. He has been running Blazor in production since it was launched by Microsoft. He is the author of *Web Development with Blazor* and the co-host of *Coding After Work* (podcast and stream).

His passion for the .NET industry and community has taken him around the world, speaking about development. Microsoft has recognized this passion by awarding him the Microsoft Most Valuable Professional award nine years in a row.

Acknowledgments

This book has been a while in the making. Not only the writing itself but also the journey leading up to it. And there are many people to whom I owe a huge thank you.

I need to start with the amazing Jessica Engström. For your kindness to a terrified conference attendee and starting me on this journey by convincing me to try my hand at public speaking and for becoming an amazing friend.

To all the speakers from Swetugg 2019 for helping me get through that first talk, I'm honored that I can call so many of you friends now.

And to Mattias Karlsson, for inviting me to write my first technical talk for your conference in 2020. That really put me on the road to making technical content and looking at new technologies – even if Covid got in the way and it had to be delivered virtually! I'd still love to give a technical talk for your user group/conference at some point.

To Cindy Velthuizen and Tom Ehren, for your support, advice, and time over the last few years as I made this journey.

A huge thanks to Jonathan Gennick for reaching out, asking me if I would be interested in writing a book, and helping me through those first stages.

To Shrikant Vishwakarma and Smriti Srivastava for your help while actually writing the book and keeping me on track.

And everyone else at Apress who make getting books from Word documents on my computer to being an actual book possible.

To my technical reviewers.

Marc Duiker for checking that I was doing the right things with the Azure Functions through the chapters, and laughter at some of the comments I made.

And Jimmy Engström for doing the same with the Blazor code and helping me think my way out of problems during the writing.

Of course, any issues that remain here are entirely down to me!

And to everyone else, too numerous to mention, who have helped me get this book into readers' hands.

ACKNOWLEDGMENTS

Finally, my parents for always supporting me in what I wanted, and needed to do, and cheering me on when it would have been so easy to give up at school, college, and university. It means the world to me that you believed in me through those years.

And my partner and child, who wish to remain anonymous, but it wouldn't be right to not include them here. For your love, support, and helping me stay on track, I am forever indebted.

PART I

Getting Started

To get an Azure Static Web App into production, we first have to do some groundwork.

There are online accounts that we need to create and set up, and there are applications that we need to install.

In this part, we are going to make sure that we have everything that we need to create our application and then make a sample application that we will use to create the Azure Static Web App.

Once we have all of this ready, we can start to work on our application itself!

CHAPTER 1

Introduction

A couple of years ago, I decided that I'd been putting off making my own website for too long. With the technology available to us, it doesn't need to be difficult or complex to develop our own space on the Web. I didn't want to run my site on a simple home page application though, I wanted to experiment with new technologies and learn new things!

With this in mind, I have used Azure Static Web Apps, with Blazor and .NET Azure functions, to develop my personal site over the last couple of years.

I've spoken at many conferences and meetups about the subject, and when I hear that someone has taken what I've said and tried something by themselves, it gives me a real buzz of excitement that I've helped someone take that step.

And so, I decided to write this book to take a beginner on their journey of discovery!

Before we get started though, a little background on the technology that we'll be using!

JamStack

A method of developing applications that is becoming ever more popular is JamStack. That is, using markup files and JavaScript to make a dynamic application that runs in a browser and then supplementing these with APIs to fetch and store data.

Splitting up our applications in this way allows us to take advantage of new ways of hosting sites. Our application is made of static files, so we no longer need a complex web server. We can simply host our files statically so that they can run inside of a user's browser.

As our back end now only serves data requests, rather than complete web pages, we can use the growing number of serverless possibilities to host our API, allowing easy deployment and scaling using technologies like Microsoft Azure Functions, Google Cloud Functions, or AWS Lambda Functions.

© Stacy Cashmore 2022
S. Cashmore, *Beginning Azure Static Web Apps*, https://doi.org/10.1007/978-1-4842-8146-8_1

When we put this together, we get a hosting model that is simple and cheap – even free – to put our application out into the world!

Over the last few years, this way of creating applications has been increasing in popularity over traditional server-side generated applications that require dedicated web servers to serve content.

BlamStack

JamStack is great for developers who use JavaScript technologies.

But there are lots of developers and development teams that use .NET with C#. Until now, the JamStack way of developing applications was closed to these developers. Front-end development in .NET was restricted to Web Forms or MVC. Both technologies have their place – but both are also server technologies, with the final HTML being served to the browser.

Then Blazor arrived! Originally released as a server technology, but with a browser technology released soon after – Blazor WebAssembly – allowing us to take advantage of using static files for our application.

Blazor WebAssembly runs on a .NET runtime compiled to run inside of a browser. Not using any special plug-ins – this isn't Silverlight for the 2020s – but using the built-in WebAssembly runtime in the browsers themselves.

Blazor WebAssembly applications run the same way as JamStack applications. The Blazor application handles the client application, running on the machine of the user themselves, while an API provides the data to make the application dynamic. JamStack but with Blazor: BlamStack!

Now we can take advantage of the paradigm using C# and .NET.

Azure Static Web Apps

To deploy either a JamStack or BlamStack application, there are a few components that we need to have available:

- The static file hosting for the front-end application

- Serverless functions for the API

- Routing components to connect the API securely to the front end

There are several ways to do this and with multiple providers. In 2021, Microsoft introduced Azure Static Web Apps to make this possible in Azure.

Rather than deal with each of the components that make our application separately, Azure Static Web Apps contain components all in one easy-to-manage resource.

The Azure Static Web App handles the global distribution of the static content and even handles cache invalidation when a new version of the application is deployed.

They also have built-in Azure Functions to handle the API for our application. Not only does this mean that we only need one Azure resource to handle storage, distribution, and our Azure Functions, etc., but it also connects the static content to those Azure Functions so that, to the outside world, it seems like it is one single resource. This, again, simplifies our workflow by ensuring that we do not need to handle CORS requests between the front end and back end.

And to make life even easier for us, we even get authentication out of the box with several popular platforms, meaning that we can authenticate our users without ever knowing their passwords!

If deploying from GitHub or Azure DevOps, we even get a simple continuous integration and delivery (CI/CD) flow created at the same time as our application. The fact that this works out of the box means that anyone can have a high-quality CI/CD flow without having to invest time learning how to use those pipelines, allowing for greater focus on the application itself!

It doesn't mean that we are limited in our options though! As developers, we can take more control over our Azure Static Web App if we need to, making it also suitable for the enterprise environment.

Book Focus

On our journey through this book, we will be focusing on getting started with Azure Static Web Apps, looking at what we can do to get an application into production, with authentication.

At the end of our journey, I'll leave you with some suggestions for you to carry on your project after you have finished and allow yourself to learn even more.

The book is focused on a Windows development environment; it is possible to follow along on any platform that supports .NET development – though some software will be different to the descriptions in the books.

Let's Get Started!

So, without further ado, let's get started with our journey! Before we can start with the actual code, we'll need to make sure that we have the correct accounts and software installed.

This will be the focus of Chapter 2. In Chapter 3, we'll start with the development itself!

CHAPTER 2

Setting Up the Environment

In this chapter, we will set up our development environment and required online services so that we can create our first Azure Static Web App.

We will create the online accounts and repositories needed to host our Static Web App and source code, clone the repo to our local machine, and install Visual Studio 2022 as an IDE to develop our applications locally. We can use any edition of Visual Studio for the examples in this book, including the free Community Edition.

By the end of this chapter, we will have everything that we need, both online accounts and resources on our local machine, to be ready to create and deploy our Azure Static Web App.

- Create a Microsoft Account and Azure Subscription.

- Create a GitHub account.

- Create our GitHub repository.

- Install Git on our development machine.

- Clone the repository to our local machine.

- Install Visual Studio 2022 Community Edition for development.

If you already have all the required accounts and tools already installed and are experienced in creating repositories in GitHub, then feel free to simply create a new repository, clone it to your machine, and skip ahead to the next chapter!

© Stacy Cashmore 2022
S. Cashmore, *Beginning Azure Static Web Apps*, https://doi.org/10.1007/978-1-4842-8146-8_2

Microsoft Account and Azure Subscription

Firstly, we are going to need an Azure Subscription. Without a subscription, we will not be able to create the Azure Static Web App needed to deploy our application.

If you already have an active Azure Subscription, then proceed to the section "GitHub Account."

To create an Azure Subscription, you will also need a Microsoft Account – if you do not have one of these already, then we can create one during the process of creating an Azure Subscription.

When creating your first Azure Subscription, you receive a number of benefits, some for the first month, others for the first year.

For the first month, the most important is the free Azure credits – with a value of $200 at the time of writing. This credit has two advantages for our first steps into the world of Microsoft Azure. Not only does it allow us the freedom to experiment with different resources that could otherwise have a cost associated with them, it also acts as a spending limit for that first month to protect us from provisioning resources accidentally.

To create the Azure Subscription, go to `https://azure.microsoft.com/en-us/` and click the "Try Azure for free" button, seen in Figure 2-1.

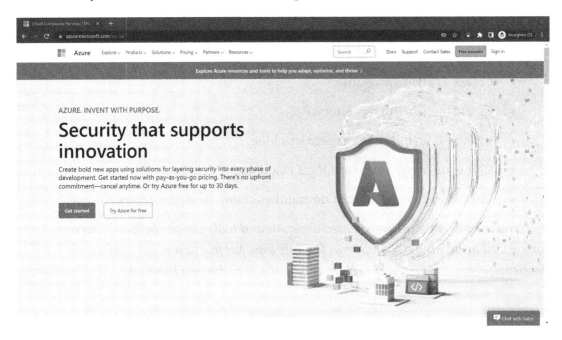

Figure 2-1. *Microsoft Azure Information Website*

This will bring us to the Microsoft Azure free trial screen. Click the green "Get started for free" button as seen in Figure 2-2.

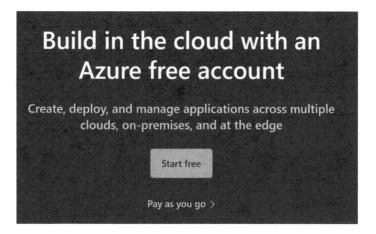

Figure 2-2. Microsoft Azure Free Trial Screen

A prompt will appear to log in to a Microsoft Account. If you do not already have an account, you can create one instead.

In the course of this flow, you will need to enter a credit card as a payment method for the subscription.

The flow to create the Azure Account asks for standard personal data (name, email, phone, address, etc.).

When the portal is visible, the account is set up and ready.

GitHub Account

Next, we need to set up a GitHub account. This will be where our code repository lives and will be used to deploy our Static Web Application into Azure.

1. Go to `https://github.com`.

2. Click the "Sign up" button.

3. In the page that opens up, enter the email and click "Continue."

4. Enter an email and click "Continue."

5. Enter a strong password.

    If the password is not strong enough, or is possibly compromised, then a message will be displayed on the page.

    Click "Continue."

6. Enter whether or not you would like to receive marketing mails and click "Continue."

The completed page will look something like Figure 2-3.

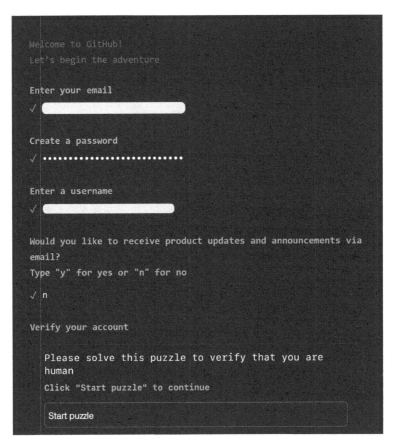

Figure 2-3. *GitHub Signup Page 1*

After completing the puzzle, GitHub will send an email with a code. This must be entered on the form seen in Figure 2-4 to prove that we have access to the email address we used.

7. Enter the code to continue the process.

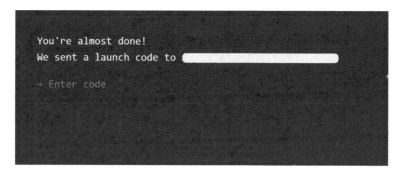

Figure 2-4. *GitHub Email Verification Code Entry*

Now the email has been verified, we can continue to set up our account!

8. Click "Just me" for the team size.

9. If you are a student or teacher, fill the information in; otherwise, leave the "Are you a student or teacher?" question empty.

10. Click "Continue."

11. We can ignore the feature selection screen for the purpose of this book.

    Click "Continue."

12. Finally, we need to select the payment plan.

    Click "Continue for free."

After selecting a plan, we will be redirected to our new GitHub dashboard as shown in Figure 2-5.

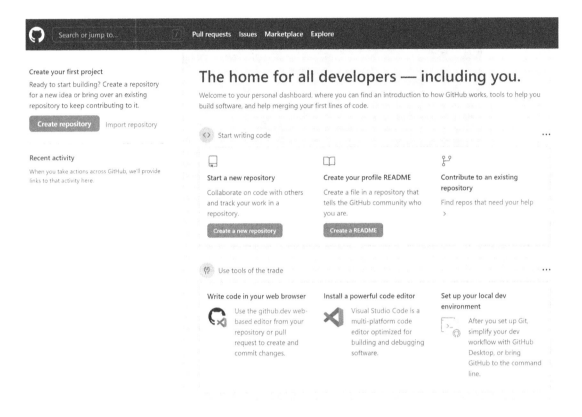

Figure 2-5. *GitHub Dashboard*

GitHub Repo

Now that we have a GitHub account, we will need to create a repository to hold our code and from where we will be building and deploying our Azure Static Web App.

From the GitHub dashboard at the end of the last session, click "Create repository" as shown in Figure 2-6.

Figure 2-6. *GitHub Create Repository Button*

This will open the screen where we enter the information needed to create a repository.

When creating a repository, it's important to check that the owner of the repository is set correctly. It should be correct by default, but it is always good to make sure!

Beyond this, there are a number of steps that we need to take to ensure that our repository behaves as expected.

Naming the Repository

Enter a name for the repository; we can use whatever name we like, as long as it is unique for the owner.

A suggestion to follow along with this book would be

"beginning-static-web-apps"

Entering a description is optional, and for now we can leave this blank. Having a good description is important however, and we can add it later.

We need to decide whether or not we would like our repository to be open for the world to see. There are advantages to having a repository marked as public. To see an overview of these, go to `https://github.com/pricing`.

There are also other advantages outside of GitHub to public repositories. They can allow us to build a public portfolio of work, to show how we develop software, for example.

Of course, there are also downsides; if we have a public repository and there is sensitive information accidentally pushed to it, then we have to assume that information is compromised and take the steps needed to protect ourselves. Though even with a private repository, we should still take care not to commit anything that could compromise our security!

To ensure that we are seeing the same behavior when accessing our repository as we see in the book, set the visibility to "private" for now. It is always possible to change the visibility at a later date.

Lastly, there are three options that we can set to initialize the repository.

Add a README File

A README file is a Markdown document explaining the purpose of the repository. This is the first documentation that people will see if our repository is public and people visit. It is displayed by default in GitHub when it exists on the home page.

README files are often used to convey the purpose of a repository, how to use the application, how to set up and run the application for development, and any extra information that could be useful.

Add a .gitignore

When creating software, many files get created which should only exist on the developer machine where they are created. Visual Studio, for example, creates files to hold user information, along with "bin" and "obj" files when code is built. These files do not need version control. Also, there are files which may contain secrets, local settings files, for instance, that we need to run code locally. These should never be pushed to a repository for security reasons.

Depending on the development language, and environment, that is used, different patterns of files should be ignored.

For this book, Visual Studio 2022 is going to be used, so we need a .gitignore tailored to that environment.

Open the drop-down box as seen in Figure 2-7.

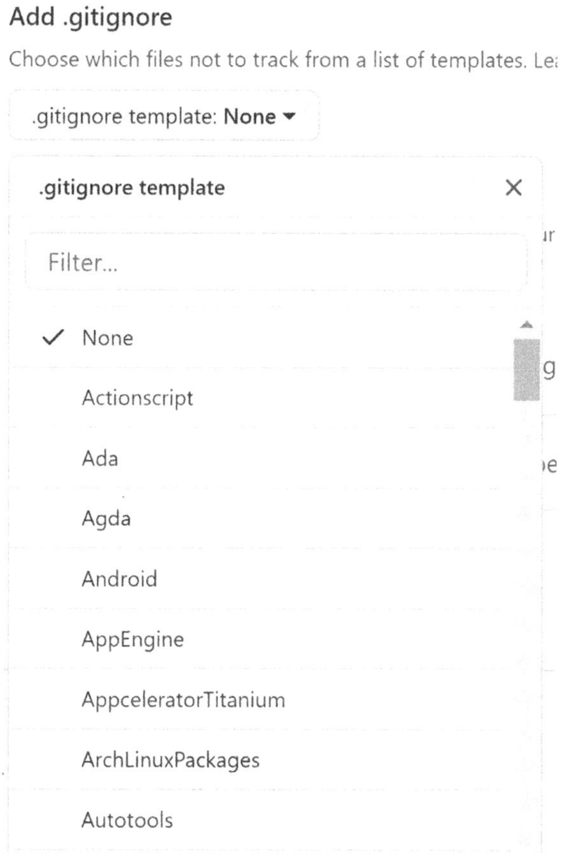

Add .gitignore

Choose which files not to track from a list of templates. Le:

.gitignore template: **None** ▾

.gitignore template	✕

Filter...

✓ None

Actionscript

Ada

Agda

Android

AppEngine

AppceleratorTitanium

ArchLinuxPackages

Autotools

Figure 2-7. *.gitignore Selection List*

As there are many options available, it is generally quicker and easier to filter the options than to search through the whole list.

Type "Visual" into the filter box, and the list will be more specific as seen in Figure 2-8.

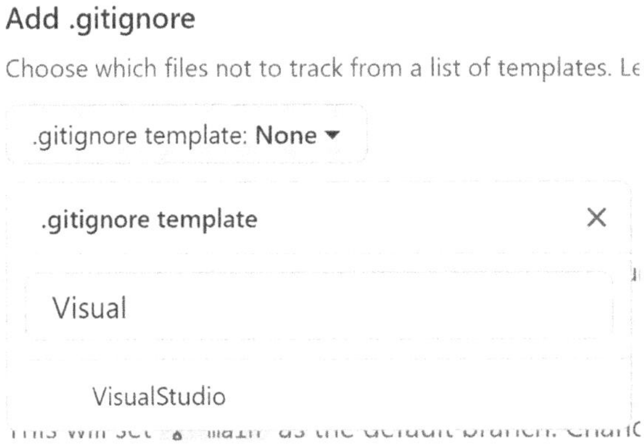

Add .gitignore

Choose which files not to track from a list of templates. Le

.gitignore template: **None** ▼

.gitignore template   ✕

Visual

VisualStudio

Figure 2-8. *.gitignore Filtered List*

Select "VisualStudio."

Choose a License

The last option is for the license used for the repository. This isn't mandatory, but if we are making a repository public, then consider adding a license to it. When we do this, it will be displayed at the top of the repository when people visit the page.

This book does not cover what license models are best – that is a choice that the repository owner needs to make. However, there are resources online that can help make the selection. For further reading, follow the following links:

https://docs.github.com/en/repositories/managing-our-repositorys-settings-and-features/customizing-our-repository/licensing-a-repository

https://choosealicense.com/

If a license is needed, select the required license from the list shown in Figure 2-9.

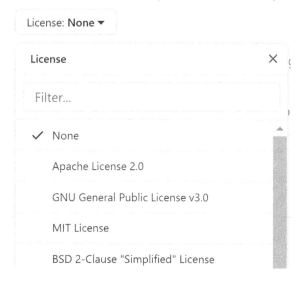

Figure 2-9. GitHub Repository License List

As with the .gitignore, we can filter the list of options to find our preferred license.

Default Branch

When the README, .gitignore, or license option is checked, GitHub will initialize the repository with a default branch in order to store those files. Extra information is displayed on the page about the default branch as seen in Figure 2-10.

This will set ⫴ main as the default branch. Change the default name in your settings.

Figure 2-10. GitHub Default Branch Explanation

Now that all options are selected, the "Create New Repository" page should look something like Figure 2-11.

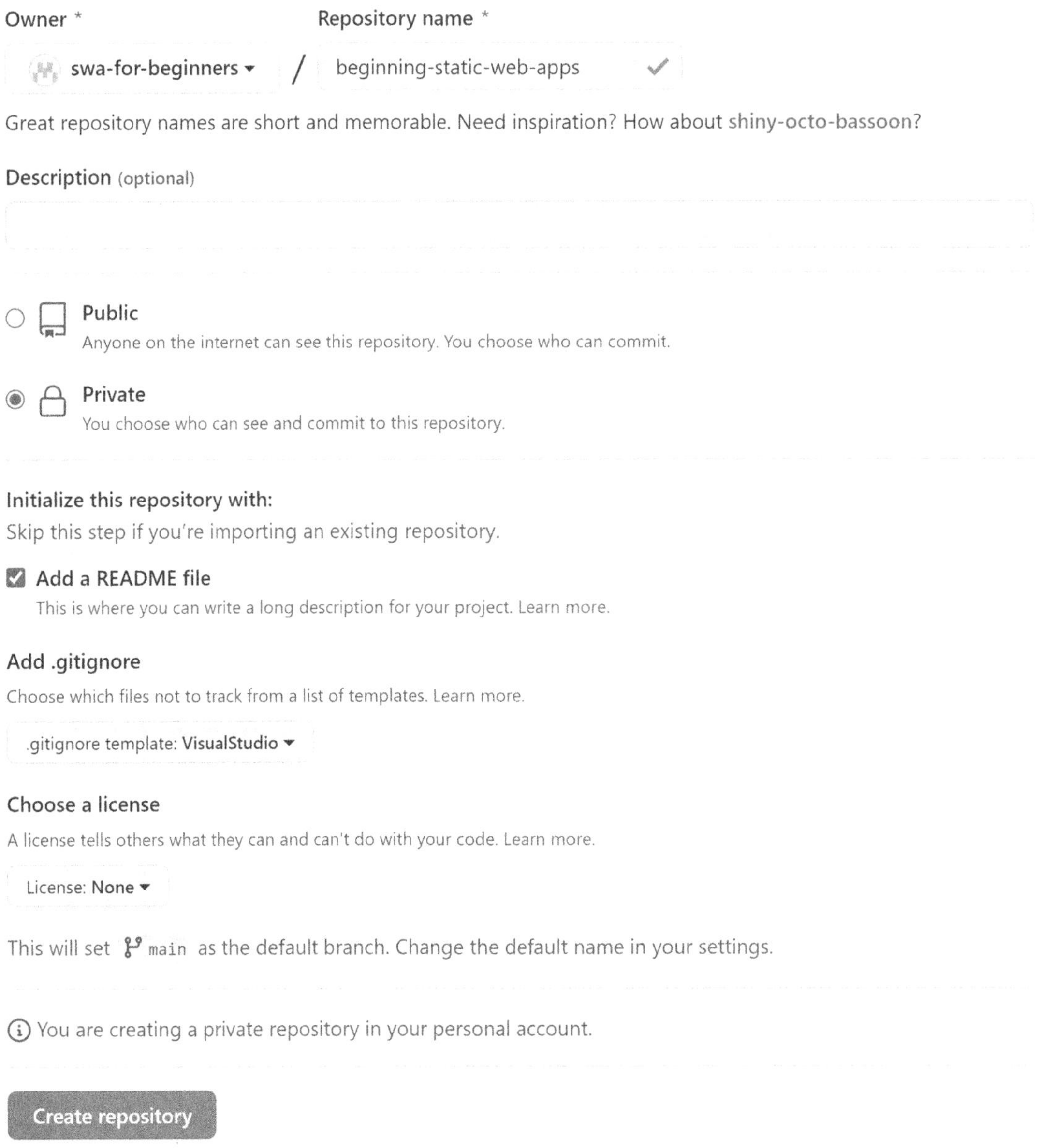

Owner *   Repository name *

🔲 swa-for-beginners ▾   /   beginning-static-web-apps   ✓

Great repository names are short and memorable. Need inspiration? How about shiny-octo-bassoon?

Description (optional)

○ 🔳 **Public**
   Anyone on the internet can see this repository. You choose who can commit.

◉ 🔒 **Private**
   You choose who can see and commit to this repository.

Initialize this repository with:
Skip this step if you're importing an existing repository.

☑ **Add a README file**
   This is where you can write a long description for your project. Learn more.

Add .gitignore
Choose which files not to track from a list of templates. Learn more.

.gitignore template: **VisualStudio** ▾

Choose a license
A license tells others what they can and can't do with your code. Learn more.

License: **None** ▾

This will set ⑂ main as the default branch. Change the default name in your settings.

ⓘ You are creating a private repository in your personal account.

Create repository

Figure 2-11. *Completed Repository Creation Page*

Click "Create repository" to complete the process.

Git

In order to use the GitHub repository for our code, we will need to clone it to our local machine. Installing Git is not complex, but there are many screens that we need to walk through during the installation.

Go to `https://git-scm.com/downloads` in a new browser tab to download the install file. For the purpose of the book walk-through, Windows is assumed – other OS installs will vary.

Once downloaded, start the install process.

1. Accept the license by clicking the "Next" button.

2. Set the install and click "Next" to continue.

3. Select the components to install.

   The defaults are fine to start with. However, it can be useful to include the Git Bash Profile for Windows Terminal, seen in Figure 2-12.

   Click "Next" to continue.

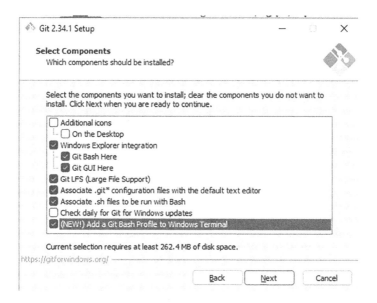

Figure 2-12. *Git Install Component Selection*

4. Select the name for the Start Menu folder; we can use the default here.

   Click "Next" to continue.

5. Choose an editor for Git.

   This is something that we won't be using in this book, but select your favorite editor from the drop-down list.

   Click "Next" to continue.

6. Choose the default name for the default branch of new repositories that we create locally.

   Again, this isn't something that we will be using in the book, but a good rule of thumb is to override the default with "main" (this is also the default alternative suggested by the installer) to make our repositories more inclusive, as seen in Figure 2-13.

   Click "Next" to continue.

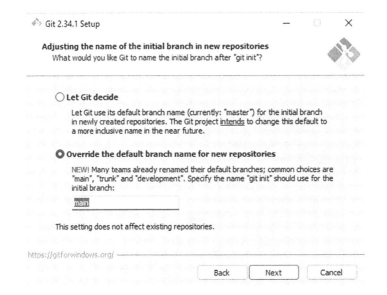

Figure 2-13. *Git Default Branch Setting*

7. Select how, or if, to add the Git command line to the PATH
    variable for use in applications other than Git Bash.
    We can keep the default value for this setting.
    Click "Next" to continue.

8. Select the SSH executable used to access our repositories.
    We can keep the default value for this setting.
    Click "Next" to continue.

9. Select the line ending conversion that Git needs to use.
    *Different operating systems use different ways of marking line
    endings; if a file is edited using these two types of line endings,
    then it can be hard to track what has actually changed in the file.
    In order to help against this, Git has options to minimize cross-
    platform edits.*
    Select the "Checkout Windows-style, commit Unix-style line
    endings" as shown in Figure 2-14.
    Click "Next" to continue.

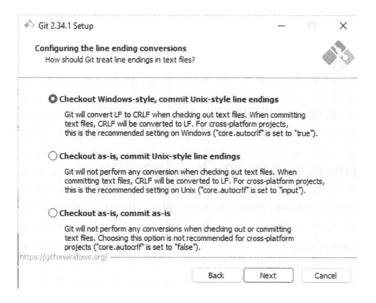

Figure 2-14. *Git Line Ending Behavior Selection*

10. Select the terminal used for Git Bash.

We will not be using the Git Bash prompt in this book and can leave this option as default.

Click "Next" to continue.

11. Select the default behavior for "git pull."

If new to git, then the default will be good enough for the exercises we have in the book.

Click "Next" to continue.

12. Choose a credential manager for Git to work with.

When communicating with remote branches, Git needs to authenticate requests. In order to make this both safe and simple, use the Git Credential Manager (the default option).

Click "Next" to continue.

13. Keep the default selection for the extra options.

Click "Next" to continue.

14. Lastly, we can choose whether to use any experimental options.

We do not need the experimental options for the examples in this book, so these can be left unchecked.

Click "Install" to continue.

Git will now install.

When the installation is complete, we can exit the installer.

Clone the Repository to Our Machine

Now that we can use Git locally, we are ready to clone the repository we created on GitHub.

Go back to the GitHub repository that we created; we should see something like Figure 2-15.

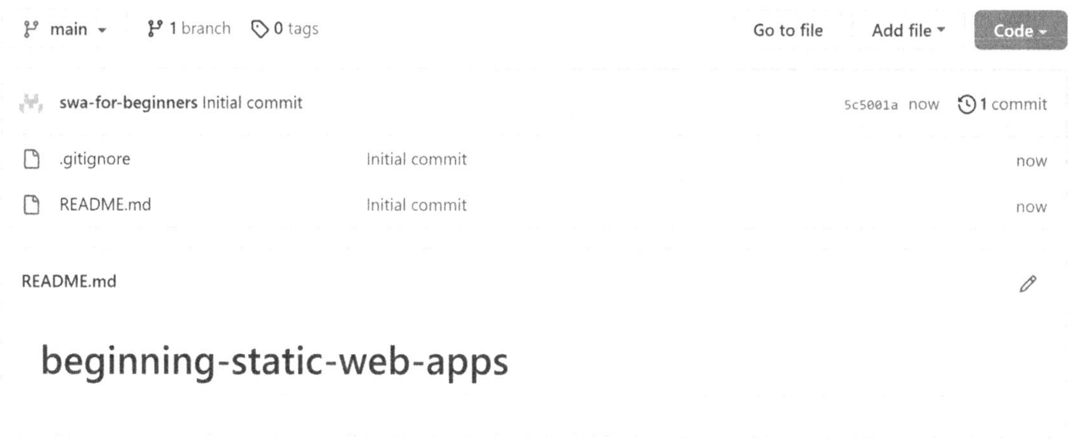
main
1 branch
0 tags
Go to file
Add file
Code
swa-for-beginners Initial commit
5c5001a now
1 commit
.gitignore
Initial commit
now
README.md
Initial commit
now
README.md
beginning-static-web-apps

***Figure 2-15.** GitHub Newly Created Repository*

Here, we can see the two files created:

- .gitignore
- README.md

The contents of the README file are also displayed under the list of files. In the top right of the screen, there is a green button "Code." Click this to expand the code context menu, as seen in Figure 2-16.

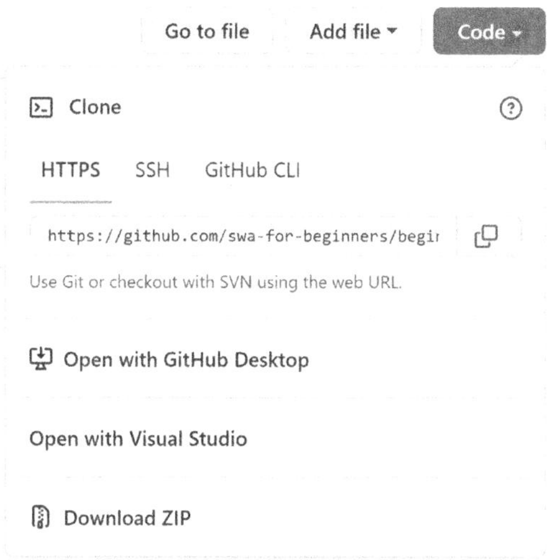
Go to file
Add file
Code
Clone
HTTPS
SSH
GitHub CLI
https://github.com/swa-for-beginners/begir
Use Git or checkout with SVN using the web URL.
Open with GitHub Desktop
Open with Visual Studio
Download ZIP

***Figure 2-16.** Expanded GitHub Code Context Menu*

In order to make a connection with the repository, we are going to clone the code to our machine using the Git command line.

Click the two overlapping squares to copy the URL for the repository, seen in Figure 2-17.

Figure 2-17. *Copy Repository URL Button*

1. Open a Terminal window.

2. Navigate to the folder that will contain our code repositories. *In the examples, "c:\github" is used as the base folder.*

3. Run the git clone command.

   For the example repository, this would be as in Code 2-1.

Code 2-1. Example Git Clone Command

```
git clone https://github.com/swa-for-beginners/beginning-static-
web-apps.git
```

Where "https://github.com/swa-for-beginners/beginning-static-web-apps. git" is the URL of the GitHub repository.

Because we are trying to clone a private repository, we need to prove that we have the rights to access it. On the GitHub Sign-In pop-up, click "Sign in with your browser" seen in Figure 2-18.

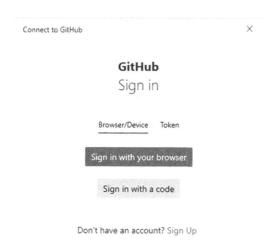

Figure 2-18. *GitHub Sign-In Pop-Up*

When the browser window opens to authorize the Git Credential Manager with GitHub, click "Authorize Git Credential Manager" as seen in Figure 2-19.

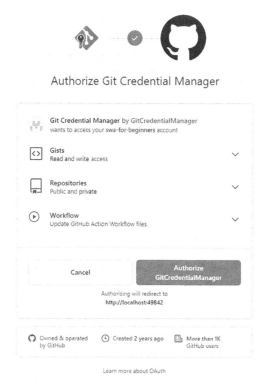

Figure 2-19. *GitHub Authorize Credential Manager*

As we are making changes to GitHub that can have security implications, we may need to reenter our GitHub password. If the pop-up seen in Figure 2-20 appears, fill in the password and click "Confirm password."

Confirm access

Password

Forgot password?

Confirm password

Tip: You are entering sudo mode. We won't ask for your password again for a few hours.

Figure 2-20. *Password Confirmation*

Git will then create a folder for the repository to be cloned into, clone the files in the repository to our machine, check out the default branch, and make a connection to the remote repository so that we can push any changes easily.

The console should look something similar to Figure 2-21.

```
PS C:\github> git clone https://github.com/swa-for-beginners/beginning-static-web-apps.git
Cloning into 'beginning-static-web-apps'...
remote: Enumerating objects: 4, done.
remote: Counting objects: 100% (4/4), done.
remote: Compressing objects: 100% (3/3), done.
remote: Total 4 (delta 0), reused 0 (delta 0), pack-reused 0
Receiving objects: 100% (4/4), done.
PS C:\github>
```

Figure 2-21. *Git Clone Result*

Visual Studio 2022

All examples used in this book will use Visual Studio 2022 as the development environment; as mentioned, all editions can be used including the free Community Edition. While this isn't a requirement for the code examples to work, there are also examples showing how we can use the development environment to help our flow. These will not work the same in other applications.

For the install examples, we are using Visual Studio 2022 Community Edition, as a paid license isn't needed to use it. If you already have a license for Visual Studio 2022, you can follow along installing either the Professional or Enterprise editions.

1. Open a browser and go to `https://visualstudio.microsoft.com/downloads`.

2. Click the "Free download," seen in Figure 2-22, to download the Community Edition.

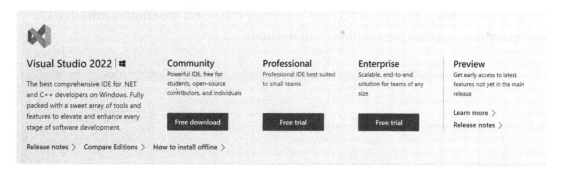

Figure 2-22. *Visual Studio Download Page*

3. Run the downloaded file.

Before Visual Studio can be installed, the Visual Studio Installer first needs to be installed. A pop-up as seen in Figure 2-23 should appear.

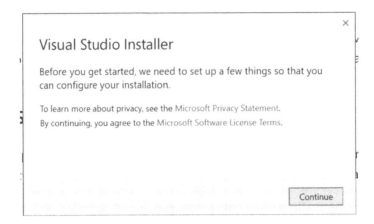

Figure 2-23. *Visual Studio Installer Start Page*

4.   Click "Continue."

Once installation is complete, the Visual Studio Installer workload selection screen is displayed, shown in Figure 2-24. This is where we can select the components that we need in order to develop the solution from the book.

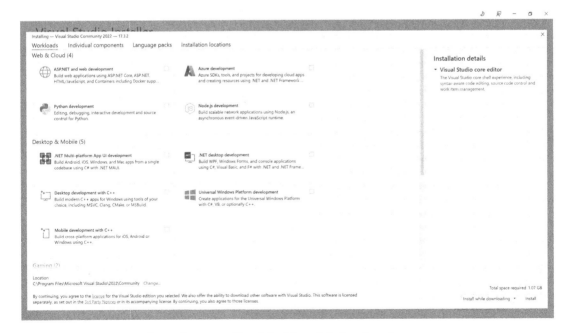

Figure 2-24. *Visual Studio Installer Workload Selection Screen*

5. Select the "ASP.NET and web development" workload. This is used for developing the Blazor Client application.

6. In the sidebar of installation details, ensure that ".NET WebAssembly build tools" are also selected.

7. Select "Azure development" workload. This is needed to develop Azure Functions inside of Visual Studio.

The selections, seen in Figure 2-25, mentioned here are the minimum needed for the examples in this book.

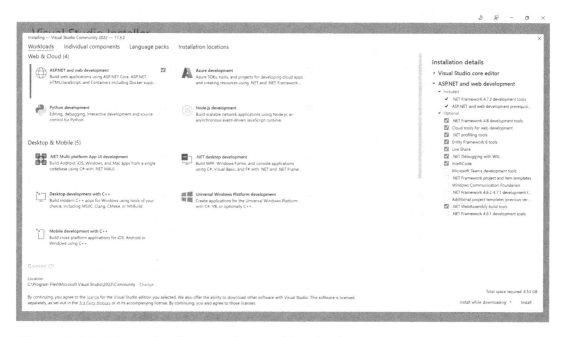

Figure 2-25. *Visual Studio Installer Workload Selection with Required Workloads/Options Selected*

8. Click "Install."

Visual Studio will now install. The time taken for the installation depends on the speed of our network connection. Progress is displayed as in Figure 2-26. Once the install is completed, Visual Studio will open. We will use this in the following chapter.

Visual Studio Community 2022 (2)   Pause

Downloaded

Installing: package 90 of 350
17%
Microsoft.CodeAnalysis.VisualStudio.Setup

☑ Start after installation

Release notes

Figure 2-26. *Visual Studio Installation Progress*

Other Languages

The examples, and project, that this book uses to demonstrate Azure Static Web Apps are written in C#, using Blazor WebAssembly, for the Client application, and .NET Azure Functions, also written in C#, for the API project.

However, using these languages is not a requirement for Azure Static Web Apps themselves. They are simply the language and technologies that have been selected.

Azure Static Web Apps support a multitude of front-end languages and frameworks that generate static files for deployment – including several static site generators. There are also many languages and frameworks supported for Azure Functions, so we are not limited to just C#/.NET here either.

If you would like to follow along using one of these languages, that is possible. The functionality of the Static Web App itself is unchanged, though accessing that functionality in code will differ extensively from the examples and project used throughout.

Conclusion

In this chapter, we have set up the cloud, and local, resources needed to get started with development. We are now ready to start developing our application! In the next chapter, we will create a base application and take a look at how to connect the front-end application to the API ready for deployment.

CHAPTER 3

Creating the Application

In the previous chapter, we set up everything that we need to get started with our application, now to make something to push to them!

In this chapter, we will create the base for the project that we will continue to expand as we work through this book.

We'll create the solution with a Blazor WebAssembly project, which will serve as our Client application. We'll add the Azure Function project that will serve as the API for the project.

We'll take a look at how both function individually, before writing code to connect the two together, by writing an HTTP function to deliver data to the client.

Finally, we will push our application to GitHub ready for the next step!

Technical Requirements

To run the examples in this chapter, Visual Studio 2022 should be installed as per the instructions in Chapter 2, and the GitHub repository created in Chapter 2 should be cloned to your local machine.

A Brief Introduction to Git

We have created a GitHub repository to host our code and installed Git on our machine so that we can interact with the repository. While we are going to be using Visual Studio for most of the interactions with Git, there are some concepts that can be useful to know.

© Stacy Cashmore 2022
S. Cashmore, *Beginning Azure Static Web Apps*, https://doi.org/10.1007/978-1-4842-8146-8_3

Clone

We used this command in the previous chapter to get the repository. The command is executed with a link to a remote repository; Git then creates a folder for that repository locally and clones it, so that it can be used locally.

This command is used before the repository exists locally.

Pull

This command is executed inside of a local repository that has already been cloned. The command will go to the remote URL where the repository was cloned from and pull any new changes into the local repository.

This is how we keep our local code up to date with changes that others have made.

Commit

This command takes changes that we have made and applies them to our repository. When we edit a file, we have what is called an unstaged change. Git is not currently tracking that change, and we can easily undo it. Once we stage a change so that Git knows about it, we can then commit it to the Git repository.

Once committed, it becomes an immutable part of the repository, with a hash referencing who changed it and when.

We need to commit changes if we want to push them to our GitHub repository.

Push

With the push command, we can take those changes that we have committed locally and push them out to the remote repository so that others can pull them down onto their machines.

This is how we share code that we have created or changed and is also how we are going to get any changes we make to our application built and deployed.

Creating the Client Application

The first project that we will create will be the client application itself. This will be a Blazor WebAssembly application that can be deployed as static files – perfect for an Azure Static Web App – that will handle all of the user interaction.

1. Start Visual Studio.

2. In the start screen that opens (see Figure 3-1), click "Create a new project."

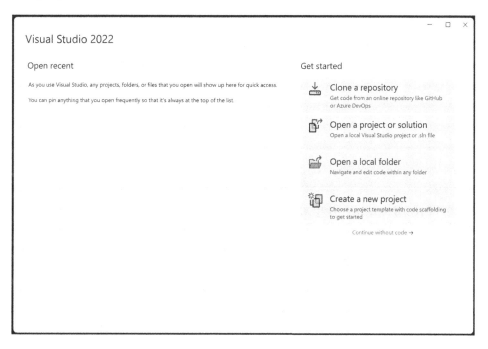

Figure 3-1. *Visual Studio 2022 Start Screen*

3. Click "Blazor WebAssembly App" (Figure 3-2).
    If "Blazor WebAssembly App" is not visible, use the search option at the top of the list.

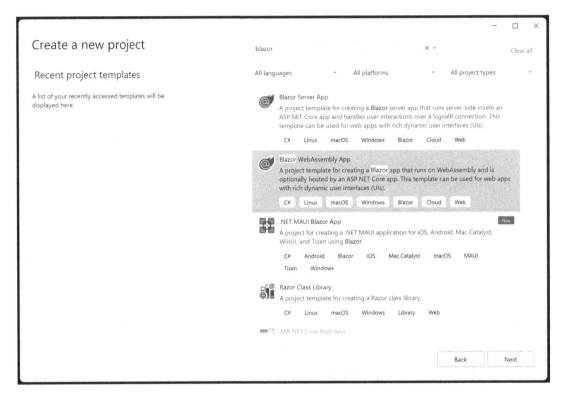

Figure 3-2. *Visual Studio 2022 Template Selection*

4. Configure the project as per Figure 3-3.

    The location should be the folder you created for all your GitHub
    repositories.

    The Solution name should be the name of the folder within that
    which contains your repository created in Chapter 2.

    *For the example in the book, the folder made for all GitHub
    repositories was "C:\github," and the repository was cloned into a
    folder called "beginning-static-web-apps."*

    Click Next when all details are filled correctly.

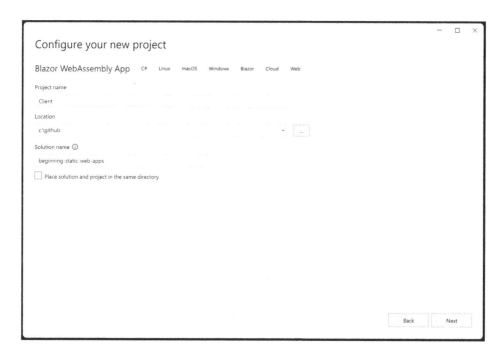

Figure 3-3. *Visual Studio 2022 Project Configuration*

5. Fill in the additional information screen (Figure 3-4).

   The fields can be left as default.

   Framework: .NET 6.0 (Long-term support)

   Authentication type: None

   We will be adding this in a later chapter.

   Configure for HTTPS: Checked

   ASP.NET Core hosted: Unchecked

   This is important – we cannot deploy static files if the application is ASP.NET Core hosted.

   Progressive Web Application: Unchecked

   We will not be looking at using the functionality provided by Progressive Web Apps in this book.

   Do not use top-level statements: Unchecked

6.   Click "Create" to scaffold your application.

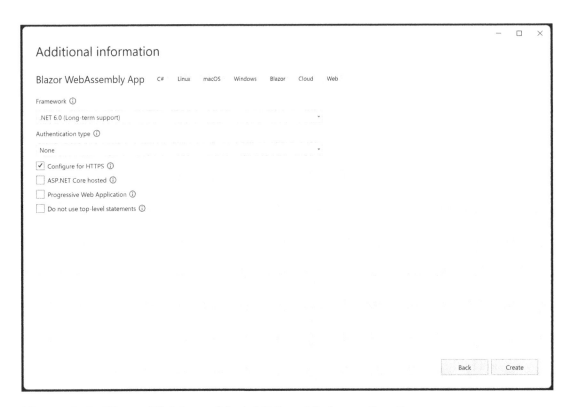

Figure 3-4. *Blazor WebAssembly Additional Information Screen*

When the page has been scaffolded, Visual Studio should load and look like Figure 3-5.

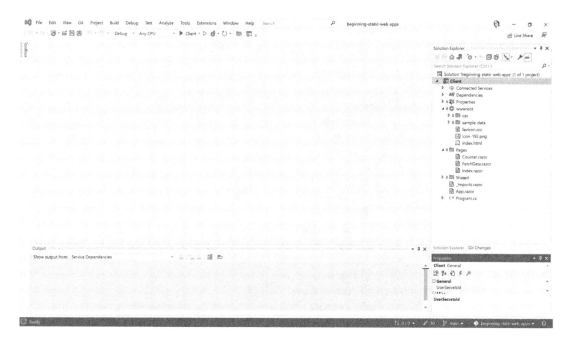

Figure 3-5. *Visual Studio 2022 After Project Creation*

Exploring the Scaffolded Blazor App

Now that our application has been scaffolded by Visual Studio, let's take a look at some of the most important files and see how they interact.

Expand the folders in the solution, by clicking the small triangle next to the folder, so that we can look at what we have available with a scaffolded solution; it should look like Figure 3-6.

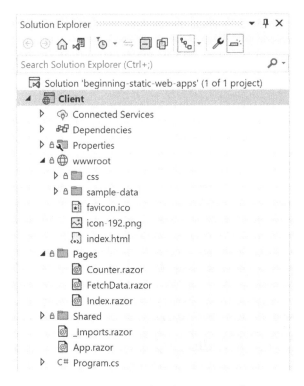

Figure 3-6. *Scaffolded Project Expanded Solution Explorer*

Application Root Folder: Client

Inside the application root folder, we have three files important for the operation of the site.

Program.cs

The Program.cs file is the entry point to our application and is run when the website is first loaded.

In this file, our WebAssembly application is created, and the App.razor component is added to the root components of the application and attached to the class "app." See Code 3-1.

To control "head" information of the HTML from within a Razor component, the HeadOutlet is added and attached to the identifier "head::after".

Code 3-1. WebAssemblyHostBuilder Creation and Root Components

```
var builder = WebAssemblyHostBuilder.CreateDefault(args);
builder.RootComponents.Add<App>("#app");
builder.RootComponents.Add<HeadOutlet>("head::after");
```

Also in this file, all services needed to run the application are initialized, including any that we need to inject into components (Code 3-2).

Code 3-2. HttpClient Services Setup

```
builder.Services.AddScoped(sp => new HttpClient ➡
  { BaseAddress = new ➡
     Uri(builder.HostEnvironment.BaseAddress) });
```

Finally, the WebAssembly application is built and run (Code 3-3).

Code 3-3. Build and Run the WebAssemblyHostBuilder

```
await builder.Build().RunAsync();
```

_Imports.razor

Each component in C# only knows about code within the same namespace as itself. To be able to use components from a different namespace, we have to tell the compiler where to look to find the code.

For namespaces that you will use often in your razor files, you can avoid cluttering every file with the same using statements by instead adding them to the "_imports.razor" file. The using statements included here will be added to each razor file automatically. We will take advantage of this later in the book!

An amount of using statements needed for most frequently are included by default when a new application is made.

App.razor

The App.razor component is where the router for the application that contains the App component is loaded (Code 3-4).

Code 3-4. Application Router

```
<Router AppAssembly="@typeof(App).Assembly">
```

This determines what razor components are loaded depending on the address of the page being loaded (Code 3-5).

Code 3-5. Router: Route Found

```
<Found Context="routeData">
    <RouteView RouteData="@routeData" ➡
        DefaultLayout="@typeof(MainLayout)" />
    <FocusOnNavigate RouteData="@routeData" Selector="h1" />
</Found>
```

The component handles loading route pages when they are found, as well as handling when a page isn't found (Code 3-6).

Code 3-6. Router: Route Not Found

```
<NotFound>
    <PageTitle>Not found</PageTitle>
    <LayoutView Layout="@typeof(MainLayout)">
        <p role="alert"> ➡
            Sorry, there's nothing at this address.</p>
    </LayoutView>
</NotFound>
```

wwwroot Folder

When a Blazor WebAssembly project is published, the wwwroot folder is copied into the published folder. This is where the static files for the client application are located.

CSS Folder

Blazor applications are created with Bootstrap (https://getbootstrap.com/) installed. The CSS files for Bootstrap, and for application-wide CSS, are created here. Isolated CSS for individual Razor components is created within the files linked to the components themselves.

index.html

This is the HTML entry point for the application. Each time the application is loaded, this page is loaded by the browser.

The static CSS files are linked as in Code 3-7.

Code 3-7. Static CSS File Links

```
<link href="css/bootstrap/bootstrap.min.css" ➥
    rel="stylesheet" />
<link href="css/app.css" rel="stylesheet" />
```

As well as the bundled isolated CSS for the Razor components (Code 3-8).

Code 3-8. Bundled CSS Link

```
<link href="Client.styles.css" rel="stylesheet" />
```

In the body of the HTML, a placeholder is made where our application will be created (Code 3-9).

Code 3-9. Div Containing a Blazor WebAssembly Locator

```
<div id="app">Loading...</div>
```

The "Loading..." will be displayed until the Blazor WebAssembly application is running.

An error section is also created for when there is a problem in the application (Code 3-10).

Code 3-10. Blazor WebAssembly Error Message Locator

```
<div id="blazor-error-ui">
    An unhandled error has occurred.
    <a href="" class="reload">Reload</a>
    <a class="dismiss">✖</a>
</div>
```

And finally, the Blazor application is called via the "blazor.webassembly.js" script at the end of the file (Code 3-11).

Code 3-11. Blazor JavaScript Tag

```
<script src="_framework/blazor.webassembly.js"></script>
```

It is good to know that this page exists, and what it does, but it isn't something that we are going to be changing during the course of the book.

Shared Folder

As the name implies, the shared folder contains code that is shared across the application. By default, there are three files here to run the scaffolded application, but only two of them are important to the scaffolded application that we are going to develop further.

MainLayout.razor

This is the default layout of the application. Each page that is loaded will use this file for the global template by default; it can be overridden.

The navigation menu is loaded into the sidebar as seen in Code 3-12.

Code 3-12. NavMenu Loaded in the Sidebar

```
<div class="sidebar">
    <NavMenu />
</div>
```

In the main section of the page, the content from the route is loaded into the @Body tag, as in Code 3-13. There is also a link to the ASP.NET documentation included before the content; as this isn't important for the running of the application, it isn't shown in the snippet.

Code 3-13. Component Output to the @Body Tag

```
<article class="content px-4">
    @Body
</article>
```

NavMenu.razor

This is the navigation menu for our application, which is loaded in the MainLayout. razor file. Each page that we have in our application has a `NavLink` component for easy navigation; an example is shown in Code 3-14.

Code 3-14. Navigation Link

```
<NavLink class="nav-link" href="" Match="NavLinkMatch.All">
    <span class="oi oi-home" aria-hidden="true"></span> Home
</NavLink>
```

This `NavLink` component not only displays the button for navigation but also matches the route currently loaded and highlights that link.

The navigation menu also has functionality to show or hide the navigation menu the page is displayed on a smaller screen. We get a responsive design by default.

Pages Folder

Now that we have seen the parts that make the application work, let's take a look at the components that bring these together to make the pages we will actually see!

Index.razor

The Index.razor is the root page of our application. This is the content that our users will see when they first visit our application. It's the place where we can link to other parts of the site and put important information for them to see as soon as they arrive.

Code 3-15. Index.Razor Component Code

```
@page "/"

<PageTitle>Index</PageTitle>

<h1>Hello, world!</h1>

Welcome to your new app.

<SurveyPrompt Title="How is Blazor working for you?" />
```

When we navigate to the root of the site, this is the page that will be served. This is controlled by the @page directive at the top of the page.

The scaffolded page sets the page title, displays the ubiquitous "Hello, world" message, and has a link to the Blazor survey.

Counter.razor

Along with the Index.razor page, there are two other pages created when we scaffold a Blazor application. The first of these is the Counter.razor.

This page shows how we can easily interact between the markup of the page that a user sees and the C# code that runs behind.

Code 3-16. Counter.Razor Component Code

```
@page "/counter"

<PageTitle>Counter</PageTitle>

<h1>Counter</h1>

<p role="status">Current count: @currentCount</p>

<button class="btn btn-primary" ➥
    @onclick="IncrementCount">Click me</button>

@code {
    private int currentCount = 0;

    private void IncrementCount()
    {
        currentCount++;
    }
}
```

The Counter page loads from the route "/counter", again set in the @page directive at the top of the page.

This page doesn't hold any exciting functionality, but it is a simple example of how to link our code to events that happen on the page. There is a button on the page, and each time it is clicked, the counter is incremented and shown to the users.

FetchData.razor

The second page that is scaffolded is the FetchData.razor page. It's an example of both how to fetch data from an API (or rather for the example, fetch data set from a JSON file on the server) and how to display lists on a page.

This is the most complex page of the scaffolded application and the most important to get a good feel of how to mix code and markup in a razor component.

Code 3-17. FetchData.Razor Component Code

```
@page "/fetchdata"
@inject HttpClient Http

<PageTitle>Weather forecast</PageTitle>

<h1>Weather forecast</h1>

<p>This component demonstrates fetching data from the ➥
    server.</p>

@if (forecasts == null)
{
    <p><em>Loading...</em></p>
}
else
{
    <table class="table">
        <thead>
            <tr>
                <th>Date</th>
                <th>Temp. (C)</th>
                <th>Temp. (F)</th>
                <th>Summary</th>
            </tr>
        </thead>
```

```
        <tbody>
            @foreach (var forecast in forecasts)
            {
                <tr>
                    <td>@forecast.Date. ➡
                                ToShortDateString()</td>
                    <td>@forecast.TemperatureC</td>
                    <td>@forecast.TemperatureF</td>
                    <td>@forecast.Summary</td>
                </tr>
            }
        </tbody>
    </table>
}

@code {
    private WeatherForecast[]? forecasts;

    protected override async Task OnInitializedAsync()
    {
        forecasts = await ➡
          Http.GetFromJsonAsync<WeatherForecast[]>➡
            ("sample-data/weather.json");
    }

    public class WeatherForecast
    {
        public DateTime Date { get; set; }

        public int TemperatureC { get; set; }

        public string? Summary { get; set; }

        public int TemperatureF => 32 + (int) ➡
          (TemperatureC / 0.5556);
    }
}
```

As well as the same @page directive at the start of the file to give the route ("/fetchdata"), there is a second directive here: @inject.

This, as the name suggests, injects an object when the page is loaded. In this case, the HttpClient object that was added to the services in the Program.cs file.

This page makes a call to a JSON file on the server, using the injected HttpClient, and then displays it in a tabular form on screen.

Running the Application

Now that we have taken a quick look at our three pages, let's see them running!

To start the application, press F5 when in Visual Studio 2022.

If it is the first time that a web application has been debugged in Visual Studio, then a message may appear asking to trust the ASP.NET Core SSL certificate (see Figure 3-7). If this appears, check "Don't ask me again" and click "Yes."

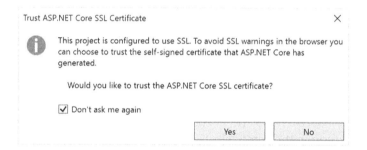

Figure 3-7. *Visual Studio SSL Certificate*

This will be followed by a Windows security warning, as we are installing a certificate from our local machine. Click "Yes" (see Figure 3-8).

Figure 3-8. *Windows Security Warning for Visual Studio SSL Certificate*

The first page that loads is the Index.razor page; see Figure 3-9. The header and navigation menu are created by the shared components in our application. The main content is from the Index.razor file. Note the URL may have a different port number (after "localhost:") than in the screenshots.

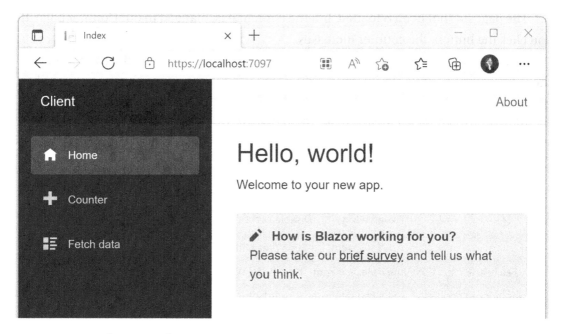

Figure 3-9. *Client Application Index Page*

Click the Counter button in the navigation menu, and the counter.razor is loaded (Figure 3-10).

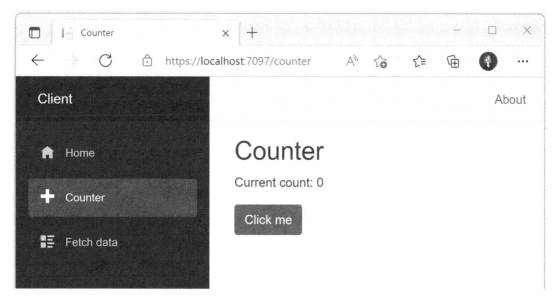

Figure 3-10. *Client Application Counter Page*

The page has not been reloaded, but the content has changed to our Counter page. If you click the button, the counter increases.

However, if you return to the Home screen and then come back to the counter page, the value of the counter is lost. Each time we navigate away from a page, the data inside of it is lost.

Before we load the Fetch data page, open the developer tools of the browser using F12 and select the Network tab as shown in Figure 3-11.

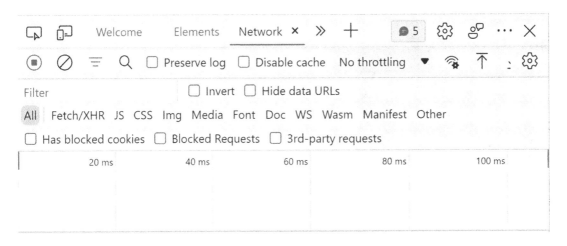

Figure 3-11. *Scaffolded Project Expanded Solution Explorer*

Now navigate to Fetch data.

As shown in Figure 3-12, there is a table containing weather forecast information. This is the data that is loaded from the sample data.

In the Network tab of the developer tools, you can see that weather.json has been loaded. Click weather.json to see more information about this call.

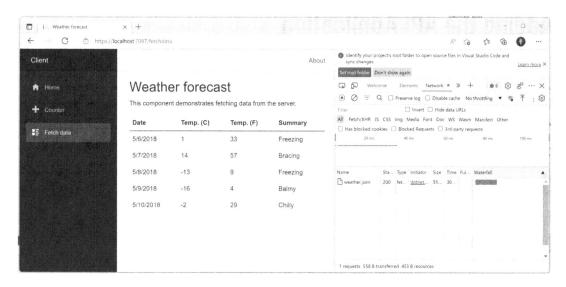

Figure 3-12. *Client Application Weather Forecast with Developer Tools*

If not already selected, click the "Headers" tab. Here, the URL of the file is shown, "sample-data/weather.json" (Figure 3-13). This folder and file can be found in the wwwroot of the application.

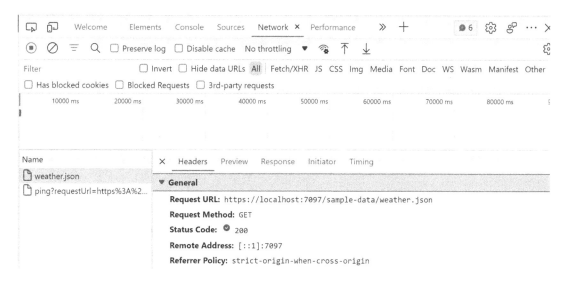

Figure 3-13. *Developer Tools Showing Request Headers for Fetching Sample Data*

Stop the debugger by closing the browser.

Adding the API Application

In order to make dynamic data available for our application, we are going to add an Azure Function to our solution. This function will be deployed alongside our Blazor WebAssembly application inside of the Azure Static Web App that we are going to make in the following chapter.

Creating the Azure Function Project

To make the Azure Function project for the API, right-click the root of the solution in the solution explorer.

1. Click "Add," followed by "New Project," as seen in Figure 3-14.

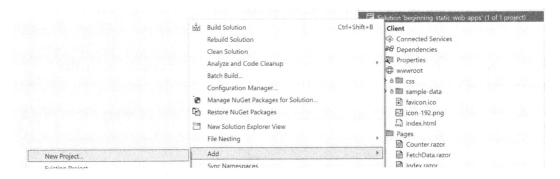

Figure 3-14. *Adding a New Project to the Solution*

2. Search for and select "Azure Functions" and click Next (Figure 3-15).

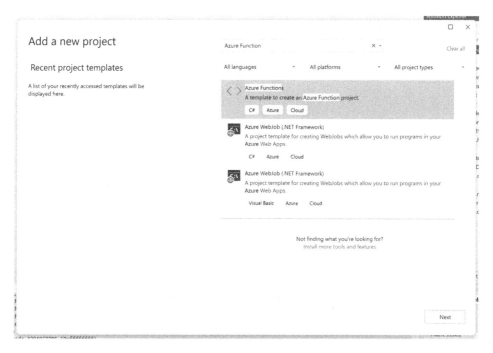

Figure 3-15. *Visual Studio Add a New Project Screen (Azure Functions)*

3. Set the project name to Api.

4. The location should be the root of your solution (in the case of Figure 3-16, "C:\github\beginning-static-web-apps").

5. Click Next.

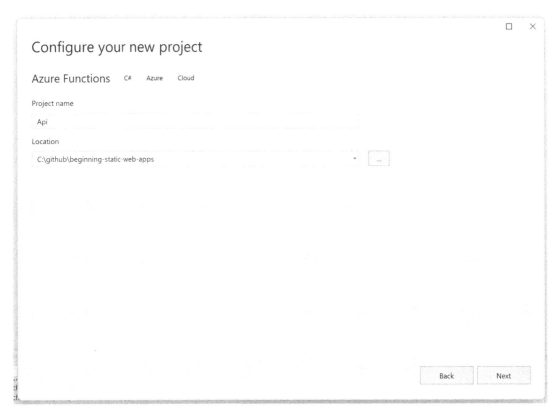

Figure 3-16. *Visual Studio Configure New Project Screen*

6. On the following screen, as seen in Figure 3-17, set the .NET version to ".NET 6.0 (Long-term support)."

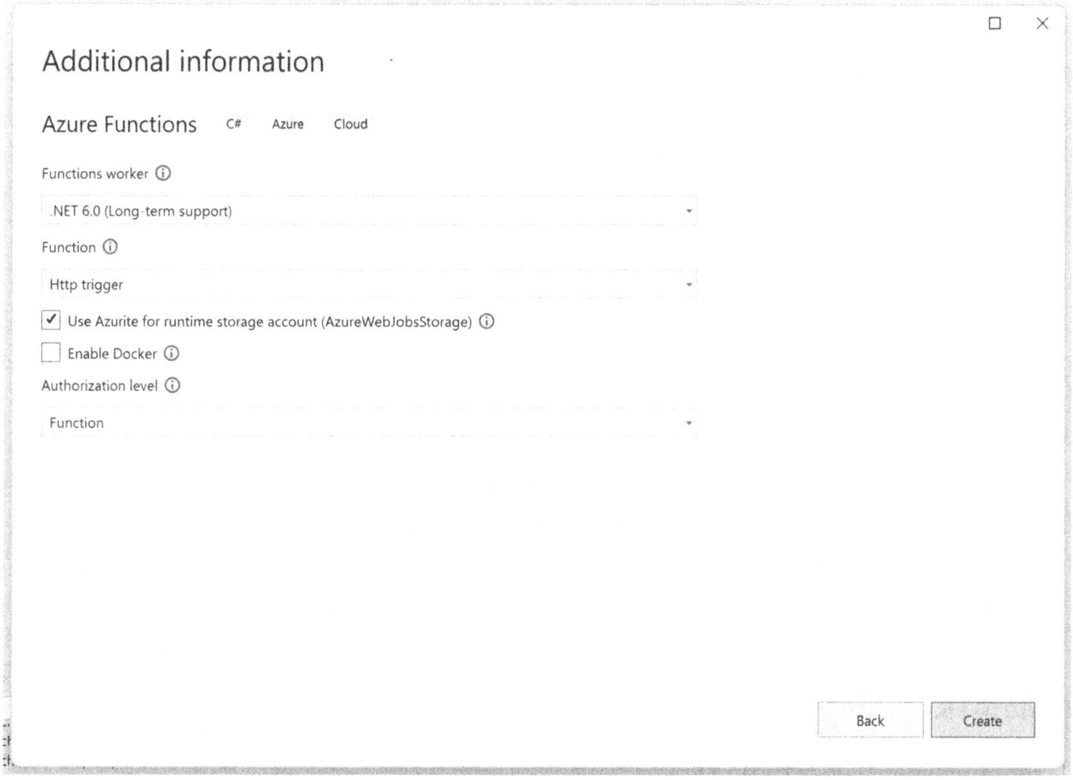

Figure 3-17. *Visual Studio Create Azure Function Screen*

7. When creating an Azure Function project, a default function can be added.

   In an Azure Static Web App, you can only use HTTP-triggered functions.

   Select "Http trigger" from the "Function" list.

8. Keep the "Use Azurite for runtime storage account (AzureWebJobStorage)" checked.

9. Keep the "Authorization level" set to "Function."

10. Click "Create."

The Azure Function project will now be created and added to the solution, similar to Figure 3-18.

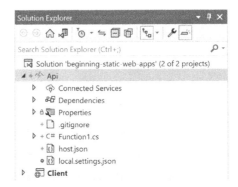

Figure 3-18. *Visual Studio Solution Explorer for the Api Project*

The Azure Function project is much simpler than the Blazor WebAssembly. There is only one file that we are going to look at before running the application: the "Function1.cs" file.

Inside the file, there is a single class "Function1." Inside this class, we have our function called "Run" with the signature seen in Code 3-18.

Code 3-18. Azure Function Http Trigger

```
[FunctionName("Function1")]
public static async Task<IActionResult> Run(
    [HttpTrigger(AuthorizationLevel.Function, ➡
        "get", "post", Route = null)] HttpRequest req,
    ILogger log)
```

This function is decorated with a "FunctionName" attribute. This marks the method as an entry point for an Azure Function. Ours is called "Function1" at the moment, the same as the class name, but it doesn't need to be.

FunctionName parameters can be any string with the limitations:

- 127 characters in length

- Start with a letter

- Only contain letters, numbers, "_", or "-"

The function parameters define this as a function with an HttpTrigger for "get" and "post" HTTP methods. As the route is "null," it will simply be the name of the function itself.

Finally, there is an HttpRequest and an ILogger passed into the function.

Inside of the function, the code checks to see if a name has been passed as a query parameter and returns some text based on that input. What it does exactly isn't important so we are not going to cover it here.

Finally, at the end of the function, the response is returned to the client as seen in Code 3-19.

Code 3-19. Azure Function Return

```
return new OkObjectResult(responseMessage);
```

Before making the changes we need for our default application, let's run the API to see the response message that is made.

Right-click the "API" project in the solution explorer (Figure 3-19); click "Debug" and then "Start New Instance."

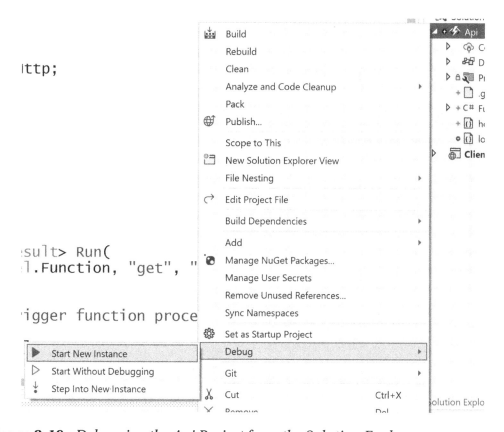

Figure 3-19. *Debugging the Api Project from the Solution Explorer*

A new command-line window should open with the Azure Functions Core Tools showing the functions found in the application. In our case, Function1, along with the URL to trigger it (Figure 3-20). As with our Blazor application, the port number may differ.

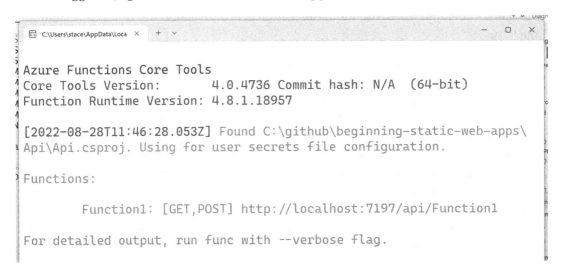

Figure 3-20. *Azure Functions Core Tools*

If a window opens for the firewall (see Figure 3-21), click "Allow access."

Figure 3-21. *Windows Firewall Security Alert*

Open a browser window at that location. The response should be as in Figure 3-22.

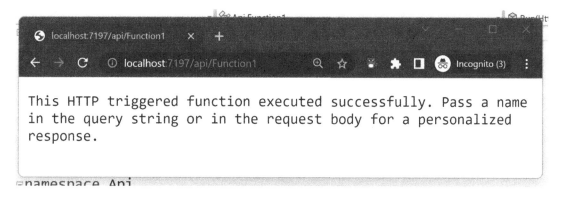

Figure 3-22. *Azure Function Result with No Input*

Now add a query string to the URL: "`http://localhost:7197/api/`
`Function1?name=beginning-static-web-apps`". The content should change to be like
Figure 3-23.

Remember to change the port 7197 to match the port seen in Figure 3-20.

Figure 3-23. *Azure Function Result with the Name Input Parameter*

Congratulations, your Azure Function project is ready for use! We can close the
Azure Functions Core Tools window to stop debugging.

Consuming the Function in the Client App

In the previous sections, we have created our Blazor WebAssembly application and
Azure Function. Now it is time to make them talk to each other!

Create a Function to Deliver the Weather Forecast

The first thing that we are going to do is add an Azure Function that will supply random weather data to replace the static JSON file that was created with the Blazor WebAssembly application.

1. Right-click the Api project and click "Add."

2. Click "New Azure Function" as shown in Figure 3-24.

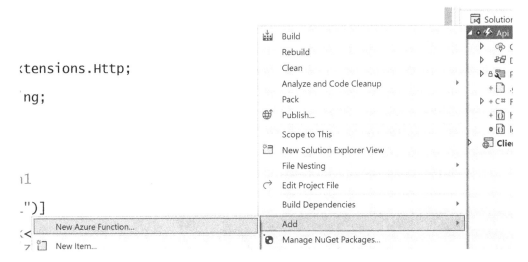

Figure 3-24. *Adding a New Azure Function to the Api Project*

3. Check that the type of file being created is an Azure Function and give it the name "WeatherForecast" as in Figure 3-25.
Click "Add."

Figure 3-25. *Add New Item Screen*

4. As when we created the default function for the project, we need to select the type of trigger for the Azure Function, though the screen is a little different.

    Pick the Http trigger as before (Figure 3-26).

    Click "Add."

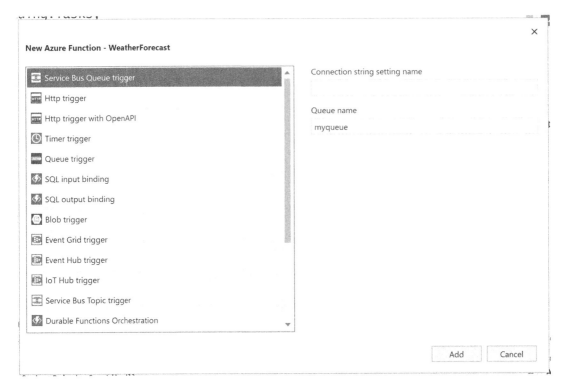

Figure 3-26. *Azure Function Trigger Selection*

A function will be created that looks the same as our first function. Replace the contents of the new file with the code from Code 3-20.

Writing the code out can help with the understanding of what it's doing. However, this code can also be found in the GitHub repository for this book if you would rather copy the code than write it out – see the end of the chapter for a link.

Code 3-20. Azure Function for WeatherForecast Sample Data

```
using System;
using System.Threading.Tasks;
using Microsoft.AspNetCore.Mvc;
using Microsoft.Azure.WebJobs;
using Microsoft.Azure.WebJobs.Extensions.Http;
using Microsoft.AspNetCore.Http;
using Microsoft.Extensions.Logging;
using System.Linq;
using System.Collections.Generic;
```

```
namespace Api;

public static class WeatherForecast
{
    [FunctionName(nameof(WeatherForecast))]
    public static async Task<IActionResult> Run(
            [HttpTrigger(AuthorizationLevel.Function,
            "get",
            Route = "weather-forecast/{daysToForecast=5}")]
            HttpRequest req, ILogger log, int daysToForecast)
    {

        return new
                OkObjectResult(GetWeather(daysToForecast));
    }

    private static dynamic[] GetWeather(int daysToForecast)
    {
        var enumerator =
                Enumerable.Range(1, daysToForecast);
        var result = new List<dynamic>();
        var rnd = new Random();

        foreach (var day in enumerator)
        {
            var temp = rnd.Next(25);
            var summary = GetSummary(temp);
            result.Add(new
            {
                Date = DateTime.Now.AddDays(day),
                Summary = summary,
                TemperatureC = temp
            }) ;
        }
        return result.ToArray();
    }
```

```
private static object GetSummary(int temp)
{
    return temp switch
    {
        int i when (i > 20) => "Hot!",
        int i when (i > 15) => "Warm",
        int i when (i > 10) => "Cool",
        int i when (i > 5) => "Cold",
        _ => "Too cold!",
    };
}
}
```

This code will create our random weather forecast. By default, for five days, but that can also be overridden in the query string to return more or fewer days if wanted.

You can test the new function is working by debugging the Api and opening the following URL in a browser, "localhost:7197/api/weather-forecast/1," remembering to replace the port number.

The JSON response should look like Code 3-21.

Code 3-21. WeatherForecast Output

```
[{"date":"2021-12-30T14:55:00.4183011+00:00"➡
,"summary":"Cool","temperatureC":12}]
```

The values for "date," "summary," and "temperatureC" will probably be different; that's fine, as long as they are in the response.

We can stop the debugger again. Our API is now ready for use!

Call the Function from the Client Application

To be able to use this code from the application, we need to make one change to our Client application. Open the "FetchData.razor" page.

Lines 42 to 45 retrieve the contents of the JSON file. Change the location of the call from "sample-data/weather.json" to "api/weather-forecast" as seen in Code 3-22.

Code 3-22. Calling Weather Forecast Azure Function from Client

```
protected override async Task OnInitializedAsync()
{
    forecasts = await ➥
        Http.GetFromJsonAsync<WeatherForecast[]>➥
        ("api/weather-forecast");
}
```

This will return the default five days of weather information. If a number is added after the weather forecast, then that number of days will be returned.

Save the file and our application is now ready for deployment!

You may have noticed that we haven't run this code locally yet to check that it works. That is because the application as it stands right now will only run inside an Azure Static Web Application. It won't run locally without extra tools or modification. We will cover this more in Chapter 5 debugging.

Pushing to GitHub

The final step that we need to take before we can create our Azure Static Web App resource is push the code to GitHub so that it's available for deploy.

1. In Visual Studio, open the "Git Changes" tab; see Figure 3-27.

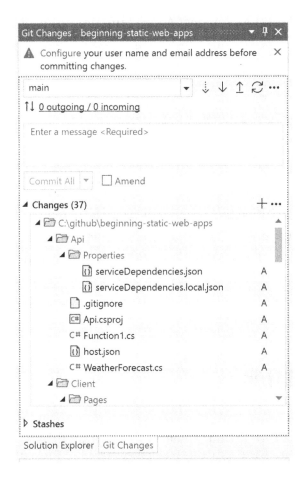

Figure 3-27. *Git Changes with Configuration Warning*

2. If you have just installed Git, then the message to configure your
    username and email address may appear at the top of the Git
    Changes tab.

    Click Configure and a Git User Information window will open
    (Figure 3-28).

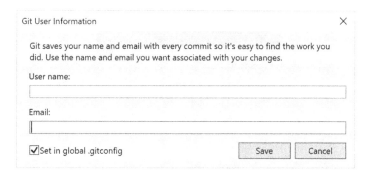

Figure 3-28. *Visual Studio Git User Information Pop-Up*

3. Fill in a username.

4. For the email, we need to return to GitHub; there is a special email address generated by GitHub to use for commits to ensure that your private email is not exposed if your repository is public (or made public in the future).

5. Open GitHub in a browser. Click your profile picture in the top right-hand corner and select "Settings" in the drop-down menu, as shown in Figure 3-29.

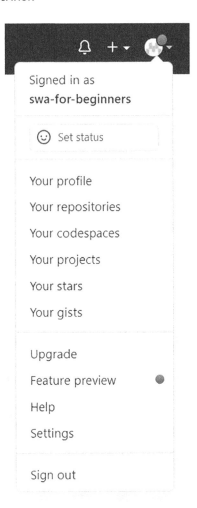

Figure 3-29. *GitHub Profile Menu*

6. In the settings page, click "Emails" and find the "Keep my email addresses private" checkbox, as shown in Figure 3-30.

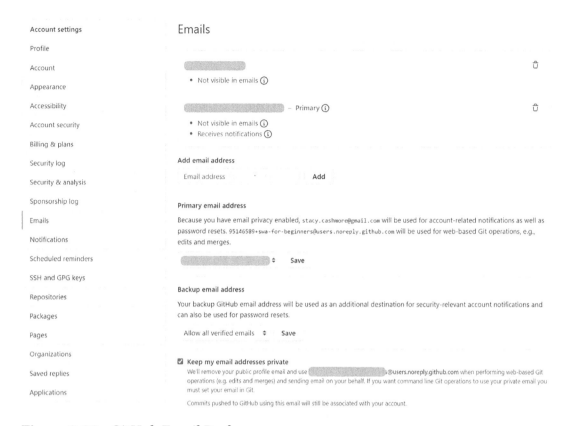

Figure 3-30. *GitHub Email Preferences*

7. If the setting isn't checked (it should be by default), then check it. Then copy the email address shown in the information text. Keep this secret, and copy it carefully – it is used to identify you when you make changes to code and push them to GitHub!

    It should be built up as the example in Code 3-23.

Code 3-23. GitHub Private Email Example

```
<number>+<GitHub Account Name>@users.noreply.github.com
```

8. Paste this into the Git User Information window (Figure 3-28).

    Click save.

9. For the message, choose something short but descriptive and keep to the present tense. For example:

   Add solution with Blazor Client and Azure Function Api

10. Click the down arrow next to Commit All.

    Click "Commit All and Push" as in Figure 3-31.

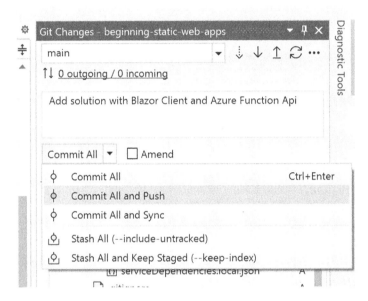

Figure 3-31. *Visual Studio Git Commit and Push Command*

Your code will then be pushed to your GitHub repository ready for the next step!

Conclusion

In this chapter, we have made the start to our application. We created our solution with a Blazor WebAssembly Application. We looked at the way the application is scaffolded by Visual Studio and how components communicate and saw it running.

We added an Azure Function project to our solution to work as our API and looked at how the HTTP trigger is wired up into the code.

We added our first function and changed the code in the Client to use the API for data rather than the static sample file.

Finally, we pushed our code to GitHub so that we can use it to create our Azure Static Web Application.

In the following chapter, we will get started with that Azure Static Web itself, creating the resource in the Azure Portal and deploying the code we just made into production!

The source code for this book is available on GitHub, located at `https://github.com/Apress/beginning-azure-static-web-apps`. For this chapter, use the "chapter-3" folder.

CHAPTER 4

Creating the Static Web App

In the previous chapter, we created our scaffolded application. We built a Blazor WebAssembly project for the client and a .NET Azure Function for our API. The next step in our journey is to create the Azure Static Web App itself and deploy our code into it!

By the end of this chapter, you will know how to create an Azure Static Web App using the Azure Portal, and you will understand how your code is deployed into it from your GitHub repository.

Technical Requirements

In order to complete the steps in this chapter, you will need to have the Azure Account created in Chapter 2 and the application from Chapter 3 available in a GitHub repository.

The source code for this book is available on GitHub, located at `https://github.com/Apress/beginning-azure-static-web-apps`. For this chapter, use the "chapter-3" folder as a starting point.

Create Resource Group

Before we can create an Azure Static Web App, we first need to have a Resource Group available to hold the resource. As the name suggests, a resource group contains a group of related resources. How the resources are grouped is up to the organization themselves; it is not prescribed by Azure.

You can learn more about resource groups here: `https://docs.microsoft.com/en-us/azure/azure-resource-manager/management/manage-resource-groups-portal`.

To create our resource group, we need to open the Azure Portal; see Figure 4-1.

© Stacy Cashmore 2022
S. Cashmore, *Beginning Azure Static Web Apps*, https://doi.org/10.1007/978-1-4842-8146-8_4

1. In a web browser, enter `https://portal.azure.com`.

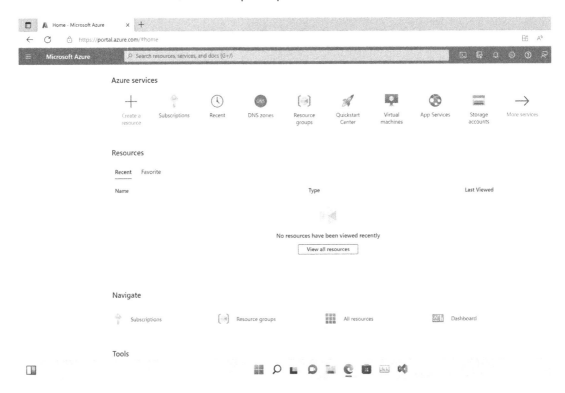

Figure 4-1. *The Azure Portal*

2. Click "Resource Groups" in the top row of "Azure Services."
    *For the new Azure Subscription created in Chapter 2, the list
    will be empty; existing subscriptions may already have Resource
    Groups listed.*

3. Click "Create resource group" or the "Create" button at the top of
    the page; see Figure 4-2.

Figure 4-2. *An Empty Resource Group Page*

To create a resource group, we need to fill in the following three fields:

- The subscription to create the resource inside of

- The name of the resource group itself

- The region where the resource group should be created

In our example, we are using "beginning-swa-rg" for the name, just to keep the naming simple and keep it recognizable to the subject of the book.

4. In the "Resource group" field, enter the name.
    There are suggestions on how to name Azure resources – and as you get more resources, these become more important to ensure that your resources are easy to manage. That is outside of the scope of the book.
    Look here if you would like to learn more: `https://docs.` `microsoft.com/en-us/azure/cloud-adoption-framework/` `ready/azure-best-practices/resource-naming.`

5. Fill in the Region for the resource group.

As I am located in the Netherlands, the example uses "West Europe."

Select the location that best matches where you are located.

A resource group stores metadata for the resources created within it. Depending on the application you are building, there may be compliance issues associated with where this is stored.

6. When the screen has been filled in, so that it looks similar to Figure 4-3, click "Review and create."

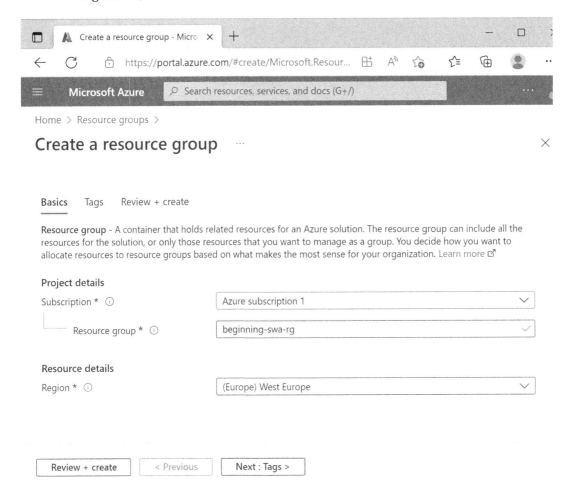

Figure 4-3. *Azure Resource Group Creation*

After validation has been completed, Azure will say whether the details entered are valid; see Figure 4-4.

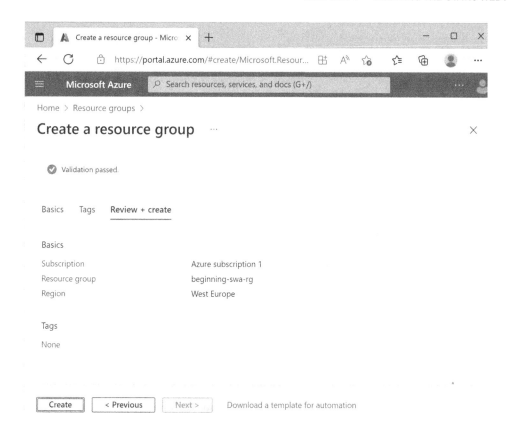

Figure 4-4. *Create Resource Group Validation Passed*

7. Click "Create."

The resource group will now be created and be visible in the Resource Group list, as per Figure 4-5.

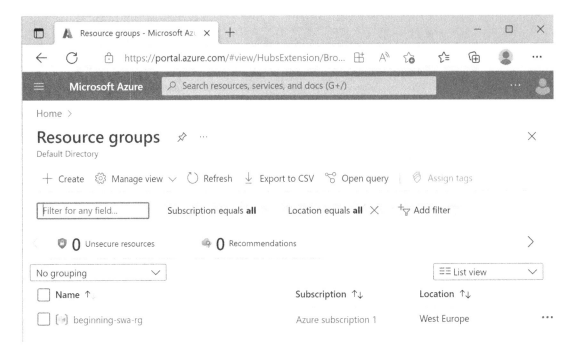

Figure 4-5. *Resource Group Created*

Click the newly created Resource Group to open it.

Create the Static Web App

Now that we have a resource group, we can use it to create our Azure Static Web App!

The process of creating an Azure Static Web App with Azure does more than simply create the Azure resource itself, at least when using GitHub as our repository. The creation process also sets up our build pipeline. So that when we make changes to our application, it is built and deployed automatically.

1. Click the "Create Resources" button in the "Resource Group" panel of the Azure Portal to start the process; see Figure 4-6.

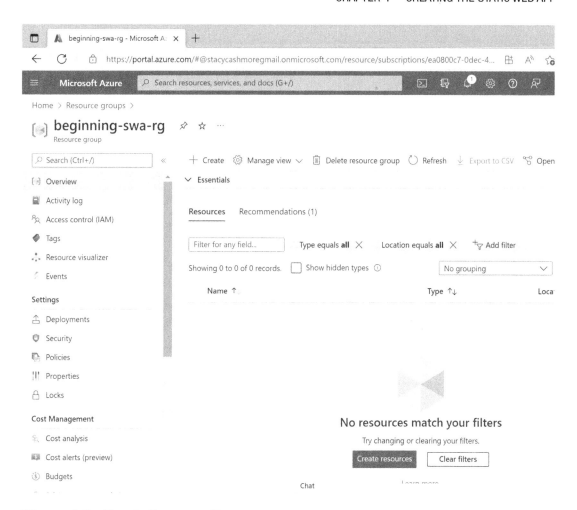

Figure 4-6. *Empty Resource Group*

The Create a Resource page will open (Figure 4-7): on the left-hand side, there is a list of categories; on the right, there are quick links for a selection of resource types; and a search box is at the top of the page to go directly to a resource type.

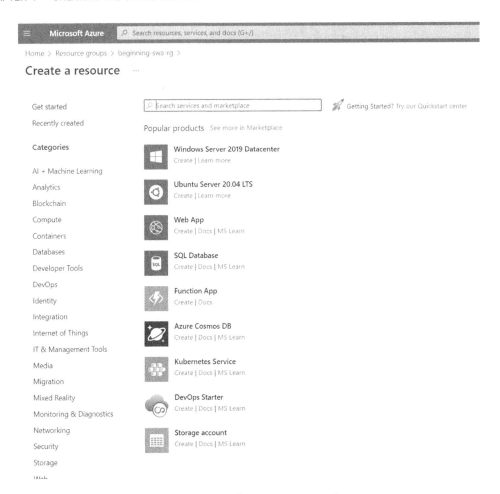

Figure 4-7. *Create a Resource Page in the Azure Portal*

2. In the search box, type "static web app."
   When we start to type in the box, it should be given to us as an
   option; see Figure 4-8.

Figure 4-8. *Search Bar and Suggestion When Creating an Azure Resource*

3. Select the "Static Web App" suggestion to open the specific resource creation page (Figure 4-9).

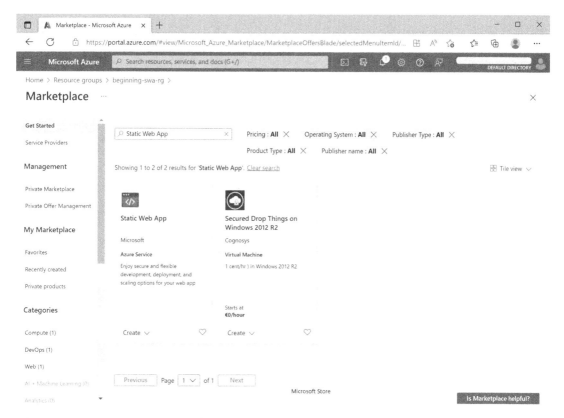

Figure 4-9. *Azure Static Web App Creation Page*

4. Click "Create" to open the resource creation page itself.

Base Information

The first information needed for our Static Web App is similar to the Resource Group itself, as seen in Figure 4-10.

Create Static Web App   ...

Basics   Tags   Review + create

App Service Static Web Apps is a streamlined, highly efficient solution to take your static app from source code to global high availability. Pre-rendered content is distributed globally with no web servers required.   Learn more ☐

Project Details

Select a subscription to manage deployed resources and costs. Use resource groups like folders to organize and manage all your resources.

Subscription * ⓘ	Azure subscription 1 ⌄
Resource Group * ⓘ	beginning-swa-rg ⌄
	Create new

Static Web App details

Name *	my-swa ✓

Figure 4-10. *Project Details for Azure Static Web Apps*

As we are creating our resource from inside of a resource group, the Subscription and Resource Group should be filled in automatically. However, it's good practice to always double-check that it is correct!

1. Check that the information for the Subscription and Resource Group are correct.

2. Enter a name for the resource group my-swa.
    In the example, "my-swa" has been picked for simplicity.

With most other Azure resources that are accessible from the Internet, the names must be unique to the whole of the Azure environment. This is because the name forms part of the URL that is assigned to the resource.

Azure Static Web Apps do not have this limitation; if the name is unique inside of the Resource Group, it can be used. The external URL is generated by Azure, which we will see later in this chapter.

3. Select the Hosting Plan for our application.
    We have two choices here: Free and Standard. See Figure 4-11.

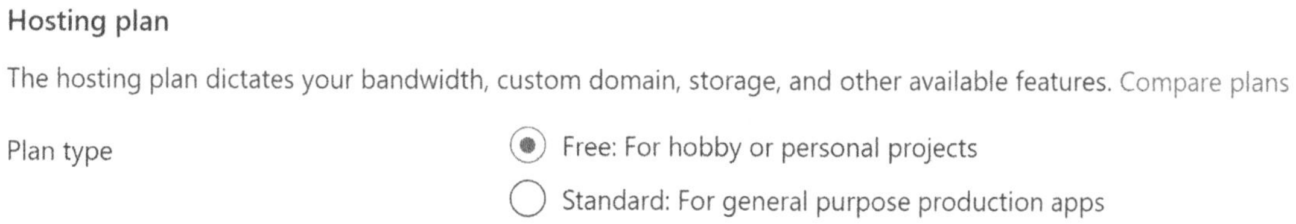

Hosting plan

The hosting plan dictates your bandwidth, custom domain, storage, and other available features. Compare plans

Plan type   ● Free: For hobby or personal projects

                             ○ Standard: For general purpose production apps

Figure 4-11. *Azure Static Web App Hosting Plan Options*

For hobby sites, and for learning about Azure Static Web Apps, the free tier is good enough. It gives the functionality that we are going to need for this book and for many applications.

For when enterprise functionality is needed, or when an SLA is important for your application, the Standard tier is available. At the time of writing, this was only around $8 per month. Even in production form, Azure Static Web Apps are a cost-effective way to get your application to production!

4. For our application, we will not be using any Standard plan options.
    Select the free plan.

If you start with the free tier but find that you need features from the Standard tier, it is possible to upscale later.

5. We need to say where our data is processed; see Figure 4-12.
    Select the required region.

Azure Functions and staging details

Region for Azure Functions API and
staging environments *   West Europe   ⌄

Figure 4-12. *Azure Static Web App Region*

As with the Resource Group, you need to consider any data compliance rules regarding data processing when picking the region for your Azure Static Web App. While the static content is globally hosted, the Azure Functions will run the region specific for the resource. On top of this, staging environments created are not globally hosted but also run in this region.

Logging In to GitHub

Now that we have set the details for the Azure Static Web App itself, we can start to define where our code is coming from.

At first glance, it can seem off that we only have two options here: GitHub and Other; see Figure 4-13. However, that comes from the tight integration between the Azure Static Web App and GitHub. At the time of writing, GitHub is the only source that includes an out-of-the-box deployment pipeline.

Deployment details

Source   ● GitHub ○ Azure DevOps ○ Other

GitHub account   Sign in with GitHub

Figure 4-13. *Deployment Details for Azure Static Web Apps*

When deploying from other sources, the deployment pipelines must be set up by hand – Azure does provide instructions for this, but it is not covered in this book:

1. Select "GitHub."

2. Click "Sign in with GitHub."

To create the necessary files and settings inside of our GitHub repository, we need to log in and authorize the Azure Portal to make changes to our repository.

After clicking "Sign in with GitHub," a pop-up will open asking for authorization; see Figure 4-14.

Authorize Azure Static Web Apps

Azure Static Web Apps by Azure-App-Service-Static-Web-Apps
wants to access your ▒▒▒▒ account

Repositories   ⌄
Public and private

Workflow   ⌄
Update GitHub Action Workflow files.

Cancel   **Authorize Azure-App-Service-Static-Web-Apps**

Authorizing will redirect to
https://portal.azure.com

Figure 4-14. *Authorization Request for Creating Azure Static Web Apps*

The rights being asked for look scary but are needed to create the workflows for deployment.

If you have previously authorized the Azure Portal, then the login screen will look slightly different.

3.   Click "Authorize Azure-App-Service-Static-Web-Apps."

Depending on how long it has been since you last entered your password, you may get a second screen asking for your GitHub password after you click "Authorize Azure-App-Service-Static-Web-Apps."

Setup for the Blazor Build

Once authorization has been given, we can select the repository that contains our code and that we want to set up the deployment flow for as per Figure 4-15.

For a standard GitHub account, the organization will be your GitHub username.

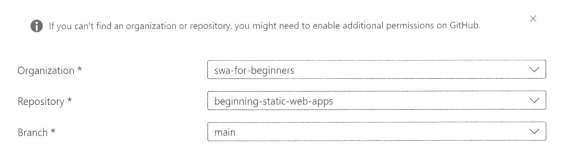

Figure 4-15. GitHub Repository Details

1. Pick the organization, repository, and branch that you have used to create the application in previous chapters.

Once the repository has been selected, we can pick the preset that we want to use for the build; see Figure 4-16.

Build Details

Enter values to create a GitHub Actions workflow file for build and release. You can modify the workflow file later in your GitHub repository.

Build Presets | Blazor   ∨ |

ⓘ These fields will reflect the app type's default project structure. Change the values to suit your app.

Figure 4-16. Blazor Build Preset

If we open the drop-down, we can see all of the options available to us:

- Angular

- React

- Svelte

- Vue.js

- Blazor

- Gatsby

- Hugo

- VuePress

- Custom

So while we are building this application using Blazor WebAssembly, it is good to know that it is not the only option available to us.

2.   Select "Blazor."

Now the final three options are available to us; see Figure 4-17.

Figure 4-17. *App, Api, and Output Location Options*

These are where we tell the build process to find the Client application (app), the Azure Functions (Api), and where the client build output can be found.

By default, and convention, these are filled in as "Client," "Api," and "wwwroot." This is the reason we named our projects "Client" and "Api" and created them in the root folder of the GitHub repository. We could have named them anything, and created them in whatever folder in the repository we wanted, but we would have also had to make sure that we corrected these settings to the locations we used. This can be useful when working in an environment with preexisting naming conventions that we need to adhere to.

The output folder, for a Blazor project at least, can be anything as long as the folder doesn't exist in the repository. Leaving it as the default is a safe option!

This is only true for Blazor websites. For other frameworks, it's far more important and must be set to the output folder of the build process for whatever framework is used.

3. Click "Review + create."

4. After the validation has completed (see Figure 4-18), click
   "Create."

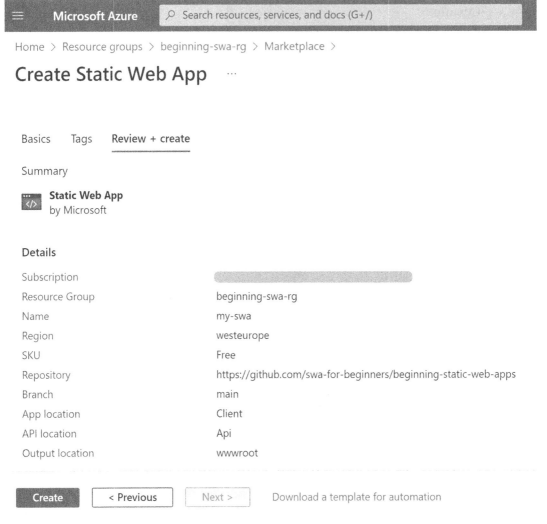

Figure 4-18. *Azure Static Web App Validation Screen*

The resource will now be created; this will take a little longer than the
resource group.

5. Once completed (see Figure 4-19), click "Go to resource" and take a look at our Azure Static Web App!

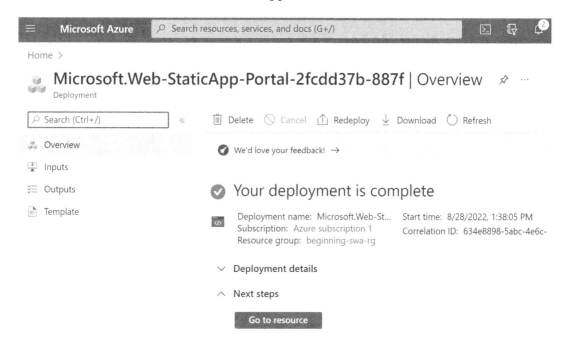

Figure 4-19. *Azure Static Web App Deployment Complete*

Later in the book, we will take a more in-depth look at the resource. At the moment, we just need to find the URL of our resource to see the app in action. On the top right-hand part of the screen, you can see the URL, as in Figure 4-20.

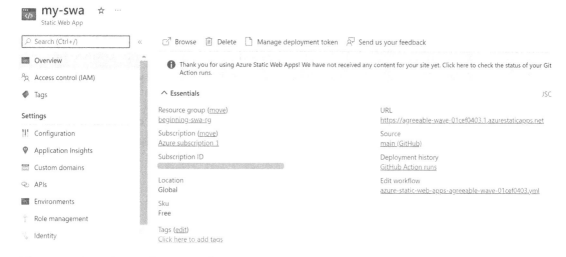

Figure 4-20. *Azure Static Web App Resource Screen*

We can see that the URL is built using an adjective, a noun, and a unique number. Azure uses these to ensure that the URL is unique, even when our resource name isn't.

Opening the New Resource

Now that the resource has been created, let's take a look at it in action!

1. Open the URL of the Azure Static Web App in a new tab.

Depending on how long it has taken from the deployment being complete to the URL being opened, you may see something similar to Figure 4-21; that isn't the Blazor client application we wanted to see!

Your Azure Static Web App is live and waiting for your content

Your app is now live, but we don't have your content updates. Check the deployment status in the GitHub Actions tab in your repository. Learn more about deployment from the Static Web App deployment docs. Learn more

Figure 4-21. *Azure Static Web App Placeholder Site*

The reason it's so empty is that Azure Static Web Apps are created very quickly, typically in a matter of seconds. However, it takes longer than that for our code to be deployed there. What is available immediately is an empty resource, with a holding page, waiting for the application!

So while we are waiting for the application to be deployed, let's take a look at how it got there. Don't close the tab with the site just yet – we'll be coming back before the end of the chapter.

Overview of the GitHub Workflow

As said, just one of the great things about Azure Static Web Apps is that if you pick GitHub as the code repository for your application, then a GitHub Workflow is created as part of the process. This gives us continuous integration and continuous delivery (CI/CD) by default. Every time our code is changed, the GitHub Workflow is triggered; our code is built and then deployed to our production environment. Automatically, without any interaction from ourselves.

If you would like to look in detail at GitHub actions, you can find more information here: `https://docs.github.com/en/actions`.

Let's check on the progress of the workflow!

1. Open a new tab in your browser and navigate to your GitHub repository.

2. Click "Actions" in the top menu; see Figure 4-22.

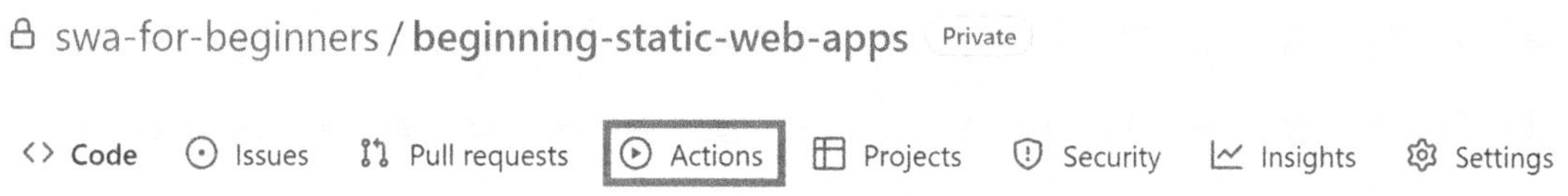

🔒 swa-for-beginners / **beginning-static-web-apps**   Private

〈〉 **Code**   ⊙ Issues   ⇄ Pull requests   ⊙ Actions   ⊞ Projects   ⛨ Security   ⤳ Insights   ⚙ Settings

Figure 4-22. *GitHub Repo Top Menu with Actions Highlighted*

Here, we can see that the workflow created by the Azure Portal is running (it may be that it has already finished); see Figure 4-23.

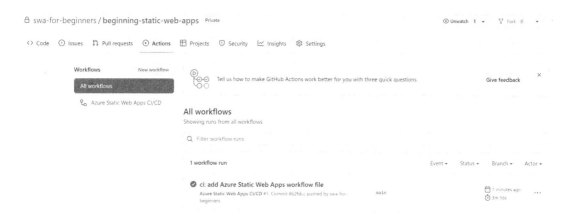

Figure 4-23. *GitHub Workflow Screen*

3. Click the "ci: add Azure Static Web Apps workflow file" to open the workflow run detail page, as seen in Figure 4-24.

Figure 4-24. *GitHub Workflow Run Details*

Workflows are built up of jobs. The workflow file that was created has two jobs associated with it. "Close Pull Requests Job," which we will look at in Chapter 12, and "Build and Deploy Jobs" which, as the name suggests, builds and deploys our Azure Static Web App for us. Click "Build and Deploy."

4. Click that job to see the details of the job itself (Figure 4-25).

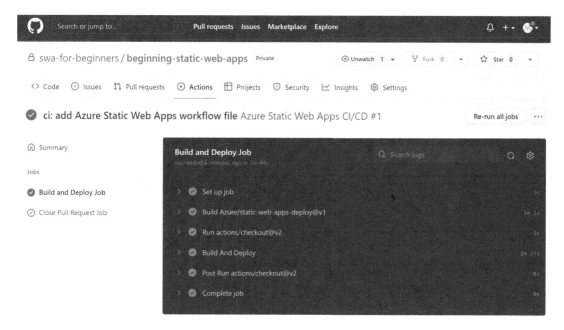

Figure 4-25. *GitHub Workflow Job Details*

A job is made of one or more actions – small, but complex, scripts that perform the steps inside of a job. Right now, this is as in depth as we are going to go – but knowing how to find this screen can be useful should you experience deployment issues!

5. Go back to the workflow screen and wait for it to turn green.

Once green, continue to the next section to look at our application in production!

If it turns red, then go back into the actions and look at the error – it could be that the "app_location" or "api_location" wasn't set correctly. In this case, look at the instructions in Appendix B.

Viewing the Deployed Application

Now that the GitHub Workflow has finished, return to the browser tab where your website was open (or open it via the Azure Portal again).

1. Refresh the page; the Blazor application should now be visible.

2. Open the developer tools, and go to the Network tab to check the change that we made to the FetchData page.

3. Click FetchData.

Check the network tab and show that the data is coming from the same URL as the client application; see Figure 4-26.

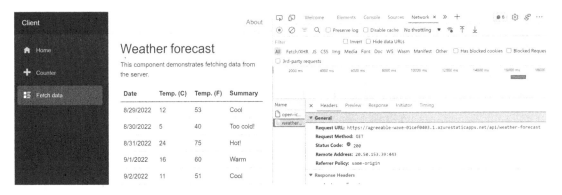

Figure 4-26. *Fetch Data with Network Tab*

If you need to revisit how to access the network tab, take a look at Chapter 3, section "Running the Application."

The fact that the data is coming from the same URL as the client application is all thanks to the glue hidden from us inside of the Azure Static Web App. This is also the reason why we could not test the application locally. When we run the code on our machine, the Client project is running on one port number and the Api project on another. We will solve this problem in Chapter 5.

There is one last thing to see before moving on to that chapter. Refresh the Fetch Data page using F5, and the site will return a 404 page (Figure 4-27). This is because the page that we are looking at doesn't exist on the server. We have deployed a Blazor WebAssembly Single Page Application. The pages themselves only exist inside of the Blazor application; they are not files served directly from the website. We will fix this problem later in the book, but it is good to be aware of this problem from the start.

← C 🔒 https://agreeable-wave-01cef0403.1.azurestaticapps.net/fetchdata

Microsoft Azure

404: Not Found

We couldn't find that page, please check the URL and try again.

Figure 4-27. *Azure Static Web App Default 404 Page*

Conclusion

In the last chapter, we created our Azure Static Web App resource that we'll be using throughout the rest of this book. We've seen the resource created in the Azure Portal and explored some of the options available to us during the process.

We've deployed our application into the resource, exploring how that happens in the GitHub action. We have seen the Client application running in a browser and that our API is now running on the same domain name as the Client and delivering the weather forecast data.

The next step in our journey will be to run the application locally, both inside of Visual Studio and by using the Static Web App CLI. We'll cover this in Chapter 5.

The source code for this book is available on GitHub, located at `https://github.com/Apress/beginning-azure-static-web-apps`. For this chapter, see the "chapter-4" folder.

CHAPTER 5

Simple Debugging

In the previous chapter, we got our simple application live, hosted inside of an Azure Static Web App and running in a production environment.

In this chapter, we will work to solve the problem mentioned at the end of Chapter 3 – that we can **only** run our application in production at the moment. By the end of the chapter, you will know how to debug inside Visual Studio, the changes needed to the code and local settings. And we'll look at using an external tool, the Static Web App CLI, to replicate the Azure Static Web App on your local machine.

By using these tools and techniques, you will be able to run and debug your application locally to enable you to quickly change and test before pushing your changes to the cloud.

Technical Requirements

To complete the steps in this chapter, you will need to have the application from Chapter 4 available in a GitHub repository and cloned to your machine.

The source code for this book is available on GitHub, located at `https://github.com/Apress/beginning-azure-static-web-apps`. For this chapter, use the "chapter-4" branch to start.

Local vs. Azure Environment

Before we start with the code, let's revisit why we have a problem running the existing code locally and take a quick look at the makeup of the application again.

Our demo application is actually made of two separate projects, which run in different frameworks and locations. Our Client application runs the front end. These are static files served from the Internet, and the Client application runs inside the browser itself.

© Stacy Cashmore 2022
S. Cashmore, *Beginning Azure Static Web Apps*, https://doi.org/10.1007/978-1-4842-8146-8_5

Then we have the Azure Functions for our API to handle dynamic data for the application. Azure Functions run in their own environment and on the server side. It is totally separate from the Client.

So, we have code running in two locations, using two frameworks, and they need to communicate with each other.

In production, the Azure Static Web App takes care of this for us. It provides the glue between the Client and the API so that to us, from the outside, they seem to be one coherent application running on the same URL.

When we run locally, we don't have that glue by default. When you run the application, the Client application will run on one HTTP port – in our test for the Client from Chapter 3, this was 7097, and the Azure Functions will run on another. In our example, this was 7197.

To debug both the front end and back end, we need to allow them to communicate with each other as they do in production!

Visual Studio Debugging

The first debugging method that we are going to use all happens inside of Visual Studio 2022. When Static Web Apps were first released in preview, this was the only way to debug applications locally. As we will see in the next section, that's no longer true – but for simpler apps, it can still be a useful way to develop.

The downside of debugging in Visual Studio is that we need to make changes to our code whose only purpose is just to allow debugging. Also, we don't have a way to debug more advanced features of the static web app, such as authentication or checking the static files themselves.

Setting the Port Numbers

Up until now, all examples have had notes to check the port numbers. To make following the examples simpler, we are going to make changes to our application to ensure that they are always predictable.

1. Open the solution in Visual Studio.

2. Right-click the "Client" project and select "Properties"; see Figure 5-1.

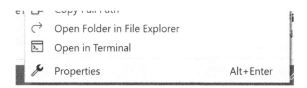

Figure 5-1. *Client Project Context Menu*

3. In the page that opens, click "Debug" on the left-hand side of the screen.

4. Click "Open debug launch profiles"; see Figure 5-2.

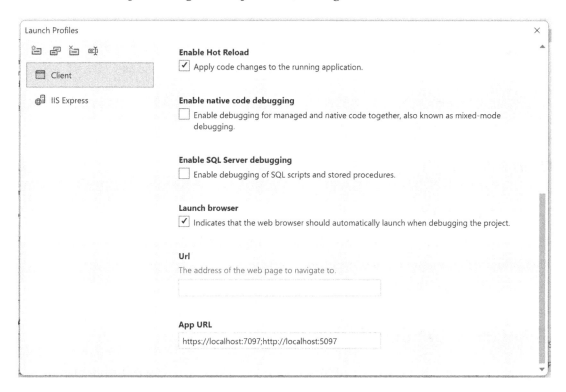

Figure 5-2. *Client Project Launch Profiles*

5. In the window that opens, scroll down to the end of the page and change "App URL" to the code from Code 5-1.

Code 5-1. App URL Entry

```
https://localhost:5000;http://localhost:5001
```

6.   Close the window.

7.   Right-click the "Api."

8.   Click "Properties."

9.   In the page that opens, click "Debug" on the left-hand side of the screen.

10.   Click "Open debug launch profiles."

11.   In the window that opens (see Figure 5-3), delete the contents of "Command line arguments" – this will reset the port of the Azure Functions back to the default of 7071.

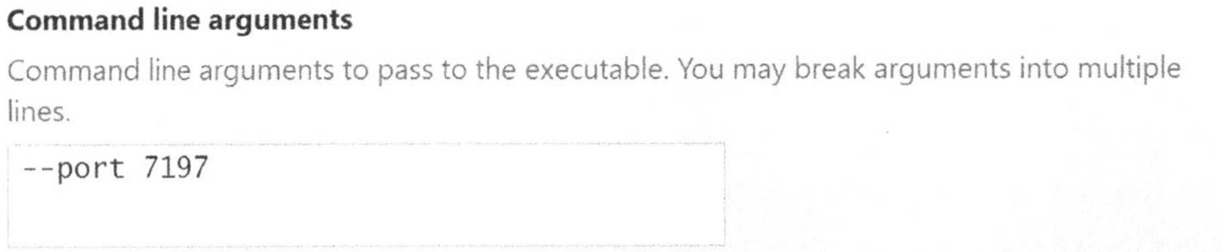

Command line arguments

Command line arguments to pass to the executable. You may break arguments into multiple lines.

```
--port 7197
```

Figure 5-3. *Api*

12.   Close the window.

If we run the application now, we should see that the Client project opens on port 5000, and the Azure Functions start on 7071.

Close all the tabs in Visual Studio but keep the solution open.

Changes to the Client Project

The Client application is currently unaware that the Api being called is hosted in a different location. Because Azure Static Web App hides some of the complexities in production, it doesn't need to. But to run it locally, those complexities come back, and we need to let it know where to find the data.

We are going to do this with the use of a local app settings file.

1.   Find the "wwwroot" folder (see Figure 5-4) in the Client project. Right-click it to open the context menu.

Figure 5-4. *wwwroot Folder in the Client Project*

2.   From the list of menu options, click "Add."

3.   From the list of menu options, click "New Item…".

4.   In the window that opens, type "json" into the search bar shown in Figure 5-5.

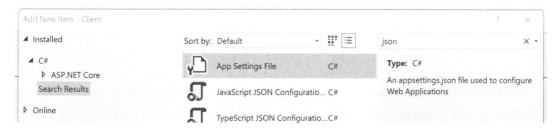

Figure 5-5. *Add New Item Search Bar – App Settings File*

5.   Select "App Settings File" from the search results, shown in Figure 5-5.

6.   Name the file "appsettings.Development.json" and click "Add."

7.   Replace the contents of the new file with the code snippet from Code 5-2.

Code 5-2. appsettings.Development.json

```
{
  "API_Prefix": "http://localhost:7071"
}
```

      8.   Open the "Program.cs" file from the Client project.

      9.   Find the HttpClient line that matches the code from Code 5-3.

Code 5-3. HttpClient in Program.cs

```
builder.Services.AddScoped(sp => new HttpClient { ➡
        BaseAddress = ➡
        new Uri(builder.HostEnvironment.BaseAddress) });
```

    10.   Replace the line with the code snippet from Code 5-4.

Code 5-4. HttpClient Setup Using builder.Configuration

```
builder.Services.AddScoped(sp =>
        new HttpClient {
                BaseAddress =
                        new Uri(builder.Configuration["API_Prefix"]
                        ?? builder.HostEnvironment.BaseAddress)
        }
);
```

The preceding steps create a local settings file; this file is only used for local development and is included in the .gitignore file. This means that it should never leave the development machine.

In this file, we created a setting that points to the base URL of the API being used by the Client application when running locally.

Finally, we use this setting when creating the HTTPClient that is injected into our Razor components and used to make HTTP calls.

By default, we try to use the "API_Prefix" setting, but if it can't be found, or is null, then we fall back to the standard base address of the Client itself being used. This would be the case when running in production.

Because we make the change when the HTTPClient is created, we only need to make this change in one location, and not each time we make a request to the API.

Changes to the Api Project

Unlike the Client project, the Api doesn't need any changes to the code itself. The problem with the Api is that in production we only want to accept requests from the same location as the Client is running; this is for security reasons.

As we have already seen, this isn't the case when running locally – so it will be seen as a different domain when making requests to the Azure Function and will fail by default. Good for production, bad for local development!

To solve this problem, we are going to add a new file to the project. This won't change the functioning of the Api in production. But it will allow us to make what are known as Cross-Origin Requests (CORS) locally.

To do this, we need to turn on CORS by changing the "local.settings.json" file. This is a file that we can use to set environment information for our local development machine. This file is only used when running locally; it will not change the way that our production application works.

1. In the solution explorer, in the root of the Api project, seen in Figure 5-6, open the "local.settings.json" file.

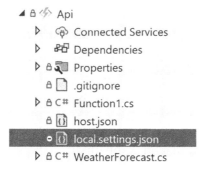

Figure 5-6. *Api Properties Folder in the Solution Explorer*

2. Change the contents of this file to match Code 5-5.

Code 5-5. Contents of "local.settings.json"

```
{
  "IsEncrypted": false,
  "Values": {
    "AzureWebJobsStorage": "UseDevelopmentStorage=true",
    "FUNCTIONS_WORKER_RUNTIME": "dotnet"
  },
  "Host": {
    "CORS": "*"
  }
}
```

This file will ensure that when we launch the Azure Functions from Visual Studio locally, it will start with CORS enabled for every origin. Not what we want in production, but perfectly safe for local development.

And that is it. We've made all of the file changes that we need to be able to run our application locally.

Running the Application

Now that we have made the changes to the code, there is only one thing left to do before running it locally.

Right now, only the Client application is set to start when we start debugging. When we wanted to run the Api in Chapter 3, we needed to debug it from the context menu in the solution for this reason.

So, we need to change that behavior so that both the Client and Api run at the same time.

1. Right-click the solution icon at the top of the Solution Explorer; see Figure 5-7.

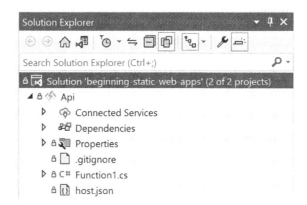

Figure 5-7. *Solution Icon in the Solution Explorer*

2. Click "Set Startup Projects."

3. In the window that opens, select "Multiple Startup Projects," seen in Figure 5-8.

4. Set both "Client" and "Api" projects to "Start"; see Figure 5-8.

5. Click "OK."

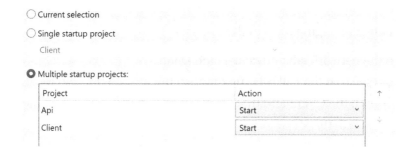

Figure 5-8. *Startup Projects Dialog Window*

That's it! Now we can run our application. Click the debug start button, or press F5. Because we changed our startup projects, three new windows should open:

- A browser with our application

- A terminal running the Client application

- A terminal running the Azure Functions Core Tools

You can see these in Figure 5-9.

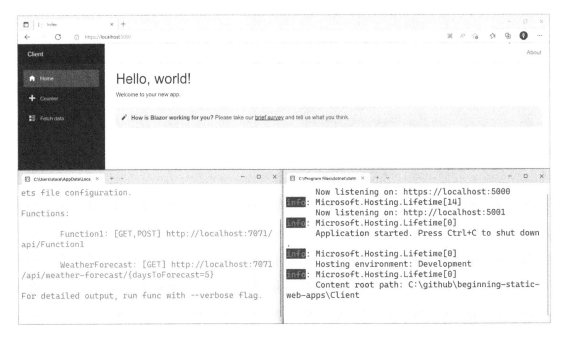

Figure 5-9. *Client Browser, Client Terminal, and Azure Functions Core Tools Terminal*

1. Open the debugging tools in the browser.

2. Go to the network tab and click Fetch Data.
   We can see that the call is being made to the Azure Function location rather than the Client and that we are getting data back as expected, as in Figure 5-10.

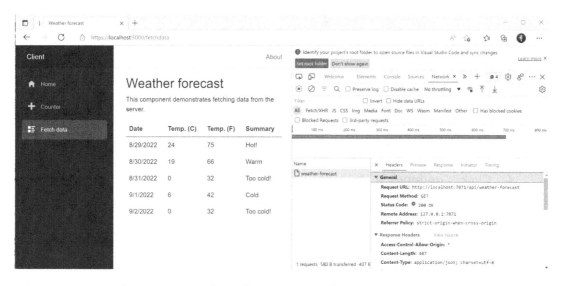

Figure 5-10. *Debugging Window Showing Weather Forecast Being Loaded*

That's how we can run our application; now to actually debug our code and see what is happening when we run the code.

Debugging the Application

When Blazor WebAssembly was released, debugging was not a simple task; the code runs in the browser, and connecting the process to the debugger was not simple. Thankfully, as .NET 6 progressed, it got easier and closer to the same experience as debugging a regular ASP.NET application.

1. While the application is running, open the "Counter.razor" file.

2. On line 16, shown in Code 5-6, press "F9" to set a breakpoint.

Code 5-6. Counter.razor Page Code Snippet

```
currentCount++;
```

3. In the browser, click the "Click Me" button of the "Counter" page. The breakpoint we just set should now be hit; see Figure 5-11.

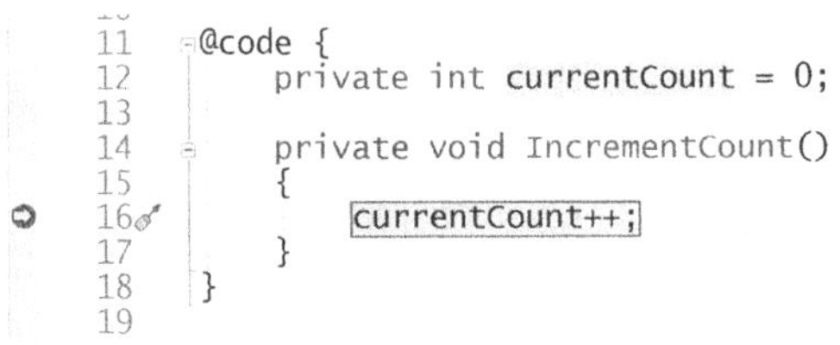

```
11    @code {
12        private int currentCount = 0;
13
14        private void IncrementCount()
15        {
16            currentCount++;
17        }
18    }
19
```

Figure 5-11. *Debug Breakpoint for "Counter.razor"*

4. Click "Continue" in Visual Studio.

Let's also do the same for the Api.

1. Open the "WeatherForecast.cs" file in the Api project.

2. On line 32, shown in Code 5-7, set another breakpoint.

Code 5-7. WeatherForecast.cs Code Snippet

```
Var temp = rnd.Next(25);
```

3. Go to the "Fetch Data" page.
    This breakpoint should be hit for each day of the forecast we have
    requested; see Figure 5-12.

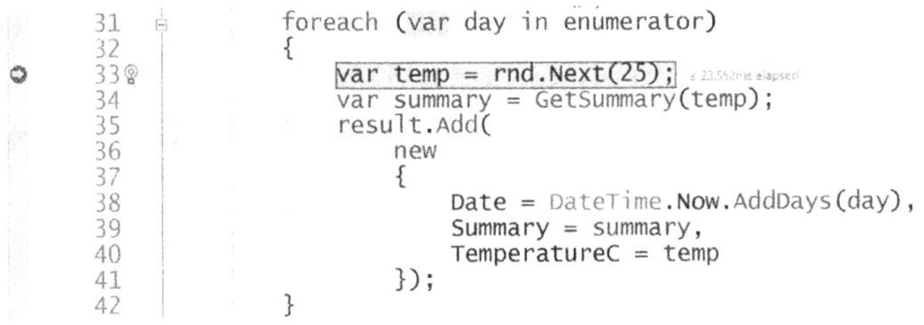

```
31        foreach (var day in enumerator)
32        {
33            var temp = rnd.Next(25);  ≈ 23.552ms elapsed
34            var summary = GetSummary(temp);
35            result.Add(
36                new
37                {
38                    Date = DateTime.Now.AddDays(day),
39                    Summary = summary,
40                    TemperatureC = temp
41                });
42        }
```

Figure 5-12. *Debug Breakpoint for "WeatherForecast.cs"*

4. Click "Continue" in Visual Studio.
    We'll need to do this multiple times as this breakpoint is in a loop.

We will come back and reuse these breakpoints later in the chapter. For now, we can
stop the Visual Studio Debugger and take a look at running our application using the
Static Web App CLI.

Static Web App CLI Debugging

If we need more advanced Azure Static Web App Features – for authentication or making our local environment behave more like the production Azure Static Web App environment – then there is a second option available to us.

We can also use this option when we only want to run our application locally, rather than have the full Visual Studio experience.

As this is the method we are going to need throughout this book, we need to undo the work we have just done in the previous section, sorry.

Resetting the Code

To reset the code manually, we need to remove the new files and stop accessing the configuration in the "Program.cs" file.

1. Delete the "appsettings.Development.json" file from the "wwwroot" folder of the Client application.

2. Delete the code from Code 5-8 from the "local.settings.json" file in the Api.

Code 5-8. Host Configuration for the Api Project in "local.settings.json"

```
,
"Host": {
  "CORS": "*"
}
```

3. In the "Program.cs" file, ensure that the BaseAddress parameter is the same as Code 5-9.

Code 5-9. BaseAddress Parameter in Program.cs

```
BaseAddress = new Uri(builder.HostEnvironment.BaseAddress)
```

If we were to try and run the application now, the "Fetch Data" will fail as the Client won't be able to find the Api. In the next section, we'll solve that problem!

The Azure Static Web App CLI

To help developers when building Azure Static Web Apps, a Command-Line Interface (CLI) is available. This is an open source application that runs on Node.js. It intercepts calls coming from the browser and redirects them to the correct location – either the Client or the Api project.

Later in the book, we will take a deeper look into this tool, to see what else it offers to help us while developing our application. But for now, we will just focus on using it to run our application and check that we can debug our code.

Install Azure Functions Core Tools

Running Azure Functions locally outside of Visual Studio requires the Azure Functions Core Tools to be installed. This will replicate the Azure Function Environment locally.

Download the tools from `https://docs.microsoft.com/en-us/azure/azure-functions/functions-run-local#install-the-azure-functions-core-tools`.

For Windows, install the 64-bit version. Click through the install wizard leaving all defaults in place.

You can read more about the Azure Functions Core Tools here: `https://docs.microsoft.com/en-us/azure/azure-functions/functions-run-local`.

Install NPM

Before installing the CLI itself, we first need to install the runtime environment needed to run it on. If Node.js is already installed, check that it and npm are up to date and proceed to the next section.

This is Node.js. Download Node.js from `https://nodejs.org/en/download/`. Pick the recommended Long-Term Support (LTS) installer for your operating system, as shown in Figure 5-13. The following install example is for a Windows 11 machine.

Figure 5-13. *Node.js Download Screen*

1. Start the downloaded installer.

2. Click "Next" on the welcome screen.

3. On the End-User License Agreement, check the license agreement and click "Next."

4. Enter the destination folder and click "Next."

5. Next, we can make changes to the features to be installed; this custom setup can be left as the defaults. Click "Next."

6. In the Tools for Native Modules window, we can leave the checkbox unchecked and click "Next."

7. That's all the options we need to check.
   Click "Install."
   A window with the install progress will now open.

8. When the "Completed the Node.js Setup Wizard" window opens, click "Finish."

Now that we have Node.js installed, we can install the Static Web App CLI itself.

Installing the Static Web App CLI

The Static Web App CLI is installed via npm, the Node Package Manager that is installed with Node.js.

1. Open a terminal window and run the command from Code 5-10.

Code 5-10. npm Command to Globally Install the Azure Static Web App CLI

```
npm install -g @azure/static-web-apps-cli
```

This command will either install the Static Web App CLI or upgrade it to the latest version if already installed.

When complete, you should have a message similar but not necessarily the same as Code 5-11.

Code 5-11. Azure Static Web App Install Result

```
added 198 packages, and audited 199 packages in 52s

32 packages are looking for funding
  run `npm fund` for details

found 0 vulnerabilities
```

The Static Web App CLI is now ready for use!

When installing the SWA, we are using the "-g" flag to install the CLI globally on our machine. If this flag is omitted, it will only install in the directory where the command is executed.

Running the Static Web App CLI

When we debug, we are going to use both Visual Studio and the CLI in tandem.

1. Start the application in Visual Studio; this will launch both the Client and Api projects.

2. Open a terminal window and go to the root directory of the application.

3. Run the command from Code 5-12.

Code 5-12. Static Web App CLI Start Command

```
swa start https://localhost:5000
```

When it has run, your terminal window should have lots of information, ending with something similar to Code 5-13.

Code 5-13. Snippet of the Static Web App CLI Output

```
[swa] Found configuration file:
[swa]    /Users/stacycashmore/code/github/stacy- ➥
       clouds.net/Client/wwwroot/staticwebapp.config.json
[swa]
[swa]
[swa] Using dev server for static content:
[swa]    https://localhost:5000
[swa]
[swa] Azure Static Web Apps emulator started at ➥
       http://localhost:4280. Press CTRL+C to exit.
```

1. Open a new browser.

2. Open the debug console and go to the network tab.

3. Browse to the URL listed in the terminal screen, normally http://localhost:4280.

4. Click "Fetch Data."
    The data should load as expected, and when we look at the request in the Network tab of the debug console, it should be coming from the same domain as the Client application. See Figure 5-14.

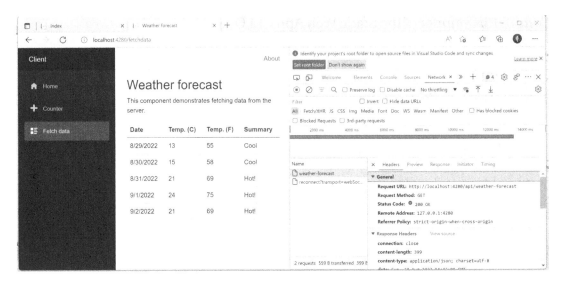

Figure 5-14. *Debug Tools Showing WeatherForecast Coming from SWA CLI*

Here, we can see the Static Web App redirecting the request to the Api for us, even while running locally!

We can also see that the API breakpoints are still being hit, so we can still debug our application in the same way as with the previous way of working.

But there is a problem with the Client application; if we try the "Click me" button on the "Counter" page, we see that breakpoint hasn't been hit. Don't worry; we'll go into detail about why this is in the next section.

Debugging the Client Using the CLI

In the previous section, we saw that by using both Visual Studio and the CLI, we can debug our API with relative ease.

But the Client application didn't work as it did when only using Visual Studio.

The reason comes down to where the code runs. Again, the API runs on a server and the Client in the browser itself.

This means that Visual Studio can easily intercept the calls to the API. The Client on the other hand is not running in an environment that Visual Studio can easily reach.

So why does it work for one and not the other?

It's the browser that was used for the request. When running only in Visual Studio, we used the browser that was opened automatically when the application was run.

Visual Studio has some clever tricks to be able to tunnel into this browser to be able to link the code to the running application.

But that is limited only to that instance of the browser. We can even see that this is a special instance of our browser – looking on the taskbar, the browser connected to our running application appears as its own icon, rather than being grouped with the other browser windows as normal. See Figure 5-15.

Figure 5-15. *Multiple Browser Icons for the Visual Studio Browser*

When we were running using the CLI, the instruction was to open a new browser. This new browser does not have the tunneling into Visual Studio, and so none of our breakpoints will be hit.

1. Open a new tab in the browser opened by Visual Studio.

2. Navigate to the `http://localhost:4280` (the CLI address) using a new tab of the browser opened by Visual Studio.

3. Navigate to the Counter page and click the "Click me" button. We should now see that the breakpoints are hit as expected.

As said at the start of this section, we are only scraping the surface of the functionality offered to us by the Static Web App CLI. But don't worry – we will return later in the book to see what other functionality it can offer us to help our developer flow!

For general development work, this is my preferred way of working. We can make changes inside of Visual Studio, and the SWA CLI will simply keep on working as its only function is to redirect the requests to Visual Studio.

Cleaning Up the Breakpoints

Before moving on, we need to remove the breakpoints so that our application doesn't keep on stopping each time we request information.

1. Stop the application in Visual Studio.

2. Open the Counter page in the Client project.

3. On the line with the breakpoint, indicated by the red dot, press F9 to remove the breakpoint.

4. Open the WeatherForecast.cs file in the Api project.

5. On the line with the breakpoint, indicated by the red dot, press F9 to remove it.

Save the Changes for the Port Numbers

The last thing that we need to do is make sure that our changes to the application to use the correct port numbers are kept.

1. Open the Git Changes tab.

2. Commit the changes to Git and push to GitHub.

The CLI and Real Azure Resource

By running the CLI, it can appear as if we have an Azure Static Web App running right there on our machine.

However, we don't. We have a Node.js server that is making it appear as though we do.

It may not sound like a significant difference, but in the course of developing our application, it is important to remember that the results we see locally may not always match what we see when we deploy our code in the real Azure resource.

As such, we should always remember to test our code in a production-like environment as well. This is also mentioned in the documentation for the Static Web App CLI.

We will cover how to do this in Chapter 12.

Conclusion

During this chapter, you have learned two techniques for running and debugging your application locally. Inside of Visual Studio for when you have a simple application and outside of Visual Studio using the Azure Static Web App CLI to be able to access more Azure Static Web App functionality during the development process.

Going forward in the book, we will focus only on the CLI method for debugging as that extra functionality will be important for us.

And with that, we have reached the end of Part 1! By following along, you have now created your first app, deployed it into production, and seen how you can debug the application for local development.

In Part 2, we will start developing our actual application. A blogging application where you can create blog posts and display them for your users.

The source code for this book is available on GitHub, located at `https://github.com/Apress/beginning-azure-static-web-apps`. For this, see the "chapter-5" folder.

PART II

Creating Our App

In the previous part, we got our development environment ready and created our first Azure Static Web App. It doesn't do much yet – we were just looking at the techniques that we are going to use to create our application.

In this part, we will make a start to the app. By the end, we will have our blog application finished to the point where people can

- See a list of blog posts

- See the latest blog post

- Read full blog posts

With these pages in place, you will have a good grounding for expanding your site to other types of content that you would like your users to have access to.

Along the way, we will look at how the Azure Static Web App resource we are using reacts to the new code that we are creating.

CHAPTER 6

Retrieving Blog Data

In our previous chapters, we have concentrated on setting up our development environment, creating the accounts that we need, installing required software, and creating our Client and Api projects and the Azure Static Web App itself.

But right now, it's just a demo site – let's change that!

First things first, we'll be cleaning up our application to remove all the demo code. Sorry, that means that we are about to delete an amount of our hard work!

Once we have our blank application, we'll add code to the Api project to retrieve information about blog posts from a CosmosDB.

Technical Requirements

In order to complete the steps in this chapter, you will need to have the Azure Account created in Chapter 2, the application from Chapter 5 available in a GitHub repository, and a deployed Azure Static Web App from Chapter 4.

The source code for this book is available on GitHub, located at `https://github.com/Apress/beginning-azure-static-web-apps`. For this chapter, use the "chapter-5" folder for the start code.

Clean Up

Let's start with cleaning the code to date. In previous chapters, we have added code to demonstrate making a call from our Client application to our Api application. This isn't something that we are going to need going forward, so we are going to remove it.

We are also going to remove the example code scaffolded by Visual Studio when we created our projects as it's not needed for the blog application that we will be making from this point onward.

© Stacy Cashmore 2022
S. Cashmore, *Beginning Azure Static Web Apps*, https://doi.org/10.1007/978-1-4842-8146-8_6

Api

There are two files in our API that we need to remove.

Delete the following files:

- WeatherForecast.cs

- Function1.cs

In the Client project, we do have a file calling the WeatherForecast API endpoint, but don't worry, we'll be removing that file as well, so this isn't going to break our application.

Client

In the Client project, there are more changes that we need to make.

1. Delete the following files:

    - Shared\SurveyPrompt.razor

    - Pages\Counter.razor

    - Pages\FetchData.razor

    - wwwroot\favicon.ico

    - wwwroot\icon-192.png

    - wwwroot\sample-data (remove the whole directory)

2. With our sample pages removed, we can also remove the navigation links to them.
   From the "Shared Folder," open the "NavMenu.razor" file.

3. We need to remove the last two entries, as shown in Code 6-1.

Code 6-1. Navigation Links to the Counter and FetchData Pages

```
<div class="nav-item px-3">
    <NavLink class="nav-link" href="counter">
<span class="oi oi-plus" aria-hidden="true"></span> Counter➥
    </NavLink>
</div>
<div class="nav-item px-3">
    <NavLink class="nav-link" href="fetchdata">
<span class="oi oi-list-rich" aria-hidden="true"></span>➥ Fetch data
    </NavLink>
</div>
```

4. From the "Shared" folder, open the "MainLayout.razor" file.

By default, there is a link to the Microsoft ASP.NET documentation. This is great when you are creating an application for the first time and want easy access to the docs, but it's not something we want in our blog application.

5. Remove the code in Code 6-2.

Code 6-2. Link to Microsoft ASP.NET Documentation

```
<a href="https://docs.microsoft.com/aspnet/"➥ target="_blank">About</a>
```

Do not remove the <div> that contains the link – we will be using this later – just remove the <a> tag.

6. From the "Pages" folder, open the "Index.razor" file.

    This is the page that is loaded by default for our application.
    When the application is scaffolded, it includes a link to a Blazor
    survey. As with the documentation link, we do not want this in our
    blog application, so let's remove it.

7. Remove the lines of code in Code 6-3.

Code 6-3. Scaffolded Index Page

```
<h1>Hello, world!</h1>

Welcome to your new app.

<SurveyPrompt Title="How is Blazor working for you?" />
```

If we run the application now, we should see that it still runs, but we now have a much emptier page – and our Counter and Fetch Data pages no longer exist.

With this housekeeping done, we can start to add to it again!

Creating the Data Source

Actually, before we do that there is one final thing that we need to do. When we finish our application, we will be returning blog posts from a data source when a user accesses our page. When we access our page, we will be able to edit and create blog posts. While it's possible to write the application faking the data, it's better to see everything working, and for that we need a data source.

Azure CosmosDB Free Tier

Azure has several ways of storing data. We are going to use an Azure CosmosDB Free Tier account. This is a cheap and simple way of storing document data, similar to MongoDB or RavenDB, and is perfect for our use case.

CosmosDB itself is out of the scope of this book. For more information on the free tier, see https://docs.microsoft.com/en-us/azure/cosmos-db/free-tier.

Create the Azure Resource

To create the CosmosDB, open the Azure Portal and go to the resource group that contains the Azure Static Web App we created previously.

1. Click the "+ Create" button.

2. Search for Azure Cosmos DB.

3. Click the Create button, as seen in Figure 6-1.

Azure Cosmos DB

Microsoft

Azure Service

Globally-distributed, multi-model
database service.

Create ∨   ♡

Figure 6-1. *CosmosDB Create Link*

CosmosDB accounts can work with different APIs, which is a different way of
accessing the data. However, each account can only have one API used for accessing the
data. So, when creating our account, we need to select the SQL API.

    4.   Click the Create button for Core (SQL) – Recommended, as in
          Figure 6-2.

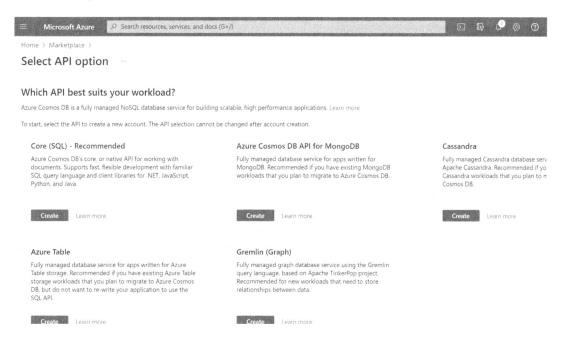

Figure 6-2. *Create Button for Core (SQL) – Recommended*

5. Check that the Subscription and Resource Group are set correctly.

6. Enter an account name; this must be globally unique; try "beginning-static-web-apps-<your name>" (see Figure 6-3).

Account Name * | beginning-static-web-apps-stacy-cashmore |

Figure 6-3. *CosmosDB Name*

7. Set a location for the CosmosDB that matches the location of your Resource Group/Azure Static Web App.

For the capacity mode, there are two options to choose from. The following instructions are assuming that this is the first CosmosDB account created for the subscription (and so we are going to use the free tier).

8. Select "Provisioned throughput" for the Capacity Mode. We need this as we are going to use the free tier.

9. For the option "Apply Free Tier Discount," choose "Apply."

10. Check the checkbox to limit the total account throughput. This will ensure that in the event of the account being used more than expected, there won't be an unexpected Azure bill.

The whole page should look similar to Figure 6-4.

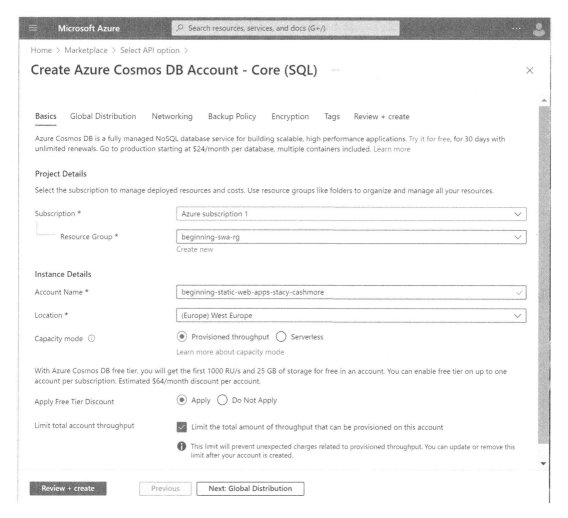

Figure 6-4. *CosmosDB Create Page*

11. Click the review and create button.

12. On the review page, double-check that the details are correct and click create.

The CosmosDB will now be provisioned.

13. Once the CosmosDB is available, go to the resource and open the Keys pane.
    Here, we can see the URI for the CosmosDB and keys for accessing the data. They should look something like Figure 6-5.

Figure 6-5. *CosmosDB URI and Keys*

For security, never share the keys to any of your Azure resources. This account has only been created for this book (by the time you are reading this, it will no longer exist) and is not in use, so sharing the keys in the book is safe.

14. Make a note of the ReadWrite URI and the Primary Key – we will be needing this in the coming section.

Seed the Table

Later in the book, we will be creating the functionality to add blog posts to the database. But to get started with retrieving blog posts, we'll seed the new database with seven blog posts.

To help do this, an application has been written which we can clone from GitHub.

1. Run the command from Code 6-4 to clone the Database seeder application.

Code 6-4. Git Clone Command for Database Seeder

```
git clone https://github.com/StacyCash/➥
    beginning-static-web-app-db-seeder
```

2. Open the "database-seeder.sln" solution.

3.   In the " DatabaseSeeding" folder, open the `DatabaseSeeder` class.

In this class, there are two variables: EndpointUri and PrimaryKey; see Code 6-5.

Code 6-5. CosmosDB Connection Variables

```
const string EndpointUri = "<Your CosmosDB Endpoint URI>";
const string PrimaryKey = "<Your CosmosDB Primary Key>";
```

4.   Replace the placeholder text, including angle brackets, for the variables with the URI and Primary Key that we copied after creating the CosmosDB.

5.   Run the application; the output should look similar to Code 6-6.

Code 6-6. Database Seeder Output

```
Created Database: SwaBlog
Created Container: BlogContainer
Cost of creating API Authorization: 10.1
Cost of creating Making your first static web app: 10.67
Cost of creating Loading From an API: 10.29
Cost of creating Navigation: 9.9
Cost of creating Setting Up The Angular Static Web App➡ Pipeline: 9.9
Cost of creating Your First Angular App: 10.1
Cost of creating Your First Page: 10.1
Blog posts seeded

C:\github\beginning-static-web-app-db-seeder\database➡
-seeder\database-seeder\bin\Debug\net6.0\database-seeder.exe➡
(process 9788) exited with code 0.
```

This application does three things:

- Create the database "SwaBlog" in the CosmosDB account.

- Create the container "BlogContainer" in the "SwaBlog" database.

- Add seven blog posts to the container for use in the coming sections.

We can now close the database-seeder solution.

Blog Post Retrieval

Now that we have a database and some blog posts to work with, let's make our application return some useful information. The first thing that we are going to add is a list of blog post summaries, so our users have a view of all blog posts on our site. We are also going to add the ability to open a single blog post.

Data Model Classes

Let's add a model to hold our blog post summary and the blog post itself. We want the summary to display a list of posts and then the actual blog post to display the full thing.

Let's look at what we want to display:

- The title of the blog post

- The author's name

- The blog post itself

- The date that it was published

- A list of tags associated with the blog post

For the summary, it's pretty much the same, the only difference being that we need to know the ID of the blog post so that we can retrieve that as well; we don't want the full blog post – for the summary, we only need to send a snippet to display with the title. However, it's close enough to the full blog post that we can use the same model for both.

Because this model is going to be shared between the Client and Api projects, we are going to add the model in a way that allows us to reuse the same code in both places. We are going to create a class library for them.

1. Open the solution in Visual Studio.

2. Right-click the solution and add a new project.

3. Search in the templates for "Class Library." Select the C# option as in Figure 6-6.

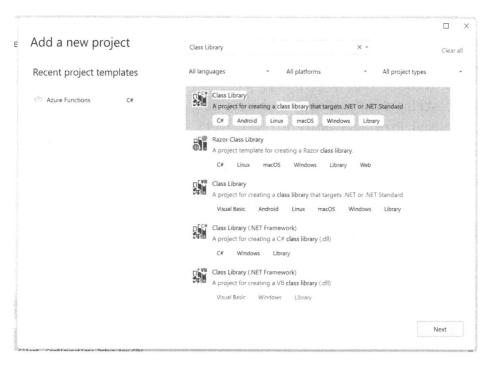

Figure 6-6. *Add a New Project Screen for Class Libraries*

4. Give the new project the name "Models" and click Next.

5. Ensure that the Framework selected is ".NET 6.0 (Long-term support)."

6. Click Create to create the new project.

7. Once the new project has been created, delete the default "Class1.cs" file.

8. Add a new class called "BlogPost."

9. Replace the content of the class with the code in Code 6-7.

Code 6-7. BlogPost.cs Model Class

```
namespace Models;

public class BlogPost
{
    public Guid Id { get; set; }
```

```
    public string Title { get; set; }
    public string Author { get; set; }
    public DateTime PublishedDate { get; set; }
    public string[] Tags { get; set; }
    public string BlogPostMarkdown { get; set; }
    public bool PreviewIsComplete { get; set; }
}
```

The model is now ready for use to retrieve our blog posts!

Retrieving Blog Post Summaries

Well, almost. We need to make the model available in the Api project.

1. Expand the Api project in the solution explorer and right-click "Dependencies," as in Figure 6-7.

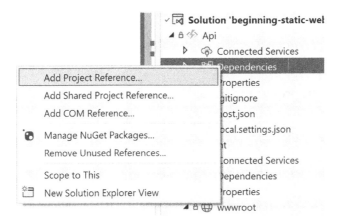

Figure 6-7. *Api Project Dependencies*

2. Click "Add Project Reference…" to open the Reference Manager window.

3. Ensure that the Models project is selected, as in Figure 6-8.

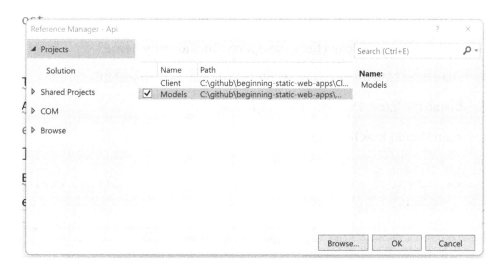

Figure 6-8. *Api Reference Manager Window*

4.   Click OK.

Now that we have the models available, we can write our first real API to get data from our CosmosDB. An Azure Function to fetch the blog post summaries for the Client!

We are going to be taking advantage of built-in Azure functionality to connect to our CosmosDB so that we have to write as little code as possible.

To do this, we need to add a NuGet package so that we can talk to the CosmosDB. In the Api project, right-click the "Dependencies" folder.

1.   Click "Manage NuGet Packages…"; see Figure 6-9.

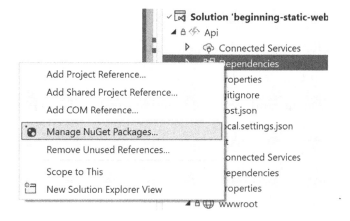

Figure 6-9. *Manage NuGet Package Context Menu for the Api Project*

2. In the NuGet Package Manager tab that opens, click "Browse."

3. Next to the search bar, check the option "Include prerelease."

4. Search for "Microsoft.Azure.WebJobs.Extensions.CosmosDB".

5. Install the latest 4.x version of the package.

The screen should look like Figure 6-10.

Figure 6-10. *Visual Studio NuGet Package Manager*

6. Click "OK" and "I Accept" if confirmation windows open.

Add a new HTTP function to the Api project; call the function "BlogPosts."

1. In the Solution Explorer, right-click the Api Project.

2. Click "Add."

3. Click "New Azure Function."

4. Name the function "BlogPosts" and click "Add."

5. Select "Http Trigger" and click "Add."

6. Open the new file and replace the contents with the code in Code 6-8.

Code 6-8. BlogPosts Azure Function

```
using Microsoft.AspNetCore.Http;
using Microsoft.AspNetCore.Mvc;
using Microsoft.Azure.WebJobs;
```

```
using Microsoft.Azure.WebJobs.Extensions.Http;
using Microsoft.Extensions.Logging;
using System.Collections.Generic;
using System.Linq;

using Models;

namespace Api;

public static class BlogPosts
{
    public static object UriFactory { get; private set; }

    [FunctionName($"{nameof(BlogPosts)}_Get")]
    public static IActionResult GetAllBlogPosts(
        [HttpTrigger(AuthorizationLevel.Anonymous,
            "get", Route = "blogposts")] HttpRequest req,
        [CosmosDB("SwaBlog", "BlogContainer",
            Connection = "CosmosDbConnectionString",
            SqlQuery = @"
                SELECT
                c.id,
                c.Title,
                c.Author,
                c.PublishedDate,
                LEFT(c.BlogPostMarkdown, 500)
                        As BlogPostMarkdown,
                Length(c.BlogPostMarkdown) <= 500
                        As PreviewIsComplete,
                c.Tags
                FROM c
                WHERE c.Status = 2")
        ] IEnumerable<BlogPost> blogPosts,
        ILogger log)
    {
        return new OkObjectResult(blogPosts);
    }
}
```

Let's look at what this code does. Firstly, you can see that the body of the Azure Function itself is empty. All we are doing is returning one value. So how does it work?

Well, this is using the Azure Cosmos integration built into Azure Functions that we just added to the project. This integration means that the connection to CosmosDB and running the query are all handled by the Azure Function. We get the results passed to us so that we can do further processing, if needed, or simply return them as the response.

The first important parameter is the "Connection" setting. When making a connection to the database, we use secrets to identify ourselves. It's vital that we do not share these secrets accidentally. Quite often, this can happen because we put connection strings or keys into code, and that code ends up in source control – as would happen with us. Then anyone with access to the source control, now or in the future, would have access to our secrets. Not what we want.

To avoid this, we will store our connection string in an external setting. When working locally, we will put this into the local settings file. Because we selected the Visual Studio .gitignore file when we created our GitHub account, this file will not be checked into our source code repository.

1. From the Api project, open the "local.settings.json".

2. At the end of the values section, add a new value as in Code 6-9.

Don't forget to replace the Cosmos URI and key with the values we copied earlier.

Code 6-9. CosmosDbConnectionString

```
"CosmosDbConnectionString": ➡
"AccountEndpoint=<Your CosmosDB URI>;➡
AccountKey=<Your CosmosDb Readwrite Primary Key>;"
```

Your final file should look like Code 6-10.

Code 6-10. Final local.settings.json

```
{
  "IsEncrypted": false,
  "Values": {
    "AzureWebJobsStorage": "UseDevelopmentStorage=true",
    "FUNCTIONS_WORKER_RUNTIME": "dotnet",
```

```
"CosmosDbConnectionString": ➡
        "AccountEndpoint=<Your CosmosDB URI>;➡
        AccountKey=<Your CosmosDb Readwrite Primary Key>;"
  }
}
```

Remember to add the setting inside the "Values" object and add a comma to the preceding line; otherwise, we'll get an error due to invalid JSON formatting.

The next parameter that we need to look at is the SqlQuery, shown in Code 6-11.

Code 6-11. CosmosDB SQL for Selecting BlogPost Summaries

```
SqlQuery = @"
  SELECT
  c.id,
  c.Title,
  c.Author,
  c.PublishedDate,
  LEFT(c.BlogPostMarkdown, 500)
      As BlogPostMarkdown,
  Length(c.BlogPostMarkdown) <= 500 As
      PreviewIsComplete,
  c.Tags
  FROM c
  WHERE c.Status = 2"
```

The SQL query selects all the fields required for the summary from our collection of blog posts, where the Status of the post is 2. This indicates that the blog post is published; we'll look at the other statuses later in the book.

Two fields are calculated – "BlogPostMarkdown" and "PreviewIsComplete." These are to select the snippet of the Post for display in the summary, rather than the full text, and to indicate whether there is more text in the blog post to recover.

Now that we have everything we need, let's try it out and see what we get back!

Run the application from within Visual Studio. Once running, open a browser and go to `http://localhost:7071/api/blogposts`. We should see a JSON list of blog post summaries. For the next part, we need to take a note of one of the IDs on the screen.

Retrieving a Single, Full Blog Post

Now that we can return a list of summaries, we also need to return a single blog post to display in full. For that, we are going to reuse the same Azure Function file but add a new method which will have a modified route.

1. Copy the code from Code 6-12 underneath the existing function.

Code 6-12. Get Single Blog Post Function

```
[FunctionName($"{nameof(BlogPosts)}_GetId")]
public static IActionResult GetBlogPost(
        [HttpTrigger(AuthorizationLevel.Anonymous, "get",
            Route = "blogposts/{author}/{id}")]
            HttpRequest req,
        [CosmosDB("SwaBlog", "BlogContainer",
            Connection = "CosmosDbConnectionString",
            SqlQuery = @"SELECT
                c.id,
                c.Title,
                c.Author,
                c.PublishedDate,
                c.BlogPostMarkdown,
                c.Status,
                c.Tags
                FROM c
                WHERE c.id = {id} and c.Author={author}")]
        IEnumerable<BlogPost> blogposts,
        ILogger log)
{
    if (blogposts.ToArray().Length == 0)
    {
        return new NotFoundResult();
    }

    return new OkObjectResult(blogposts.First());
}
```

The first thing that we'll look at is the "route" parameter. After the "blogpost" route, we now have "/{author}/{id}". That is how the function knows to differentiate routes between the two functions when a request is made. When we access the function with a blog post id and author, anything after the "/" before {author} we can use in our code.

Next is the query. This one is slightly changed from the summary query. We are retrieving the entire blog post and have lost the "PreviewIsComplete" flag. The where clause has also changed. We don't want all blog posts for this request. Rather, we only want the individual post that we have requested.

The body of the function is also a little more complex. It could be that we request a blog post that doesn't exist. The SQL query will return us an empty list in that case. But rather than return an empty list to the front end, we want to return a 404 error – not found. That is much more useful to the users of the API than an empty list.

If there are blog posts, then we return the first in the list returned from the blog posts.

Rerun the application and in a browser go to `http://localhost:7071/api/blogposts/<Author>/<id>;` replace <Author> with the corresponding author and <id> with the ID that we copied from the summary response in the previous step (or rerun the summary call and copy an ID again).

If you remove a few characters from the id and/or the author, we can check that a 404 error is returned for when a blog post can't be found.

Deploying the Functions

Now we have the functions working, we can deploy them!

1. Open the Git Changes window.

2. Check in the changes to git and push to GitHub.

Once the action has completed and the Azure Static Web App has redeployed, we can run the functions! Let's run it and see what happens.

Yes – it fails because we missed a step. When we ran the functions locally, we used the local setting file. This works for development but isn't available to our production app. As we discussed, we shouldn't be putting our secrets into our source control.

Let's add the settings in a safe way.

1. Open the Azure Portal and go to the Azure Static Web App created in Chapter 4.

2. In the left-hand pane, click Configuration, as in Figure 6-11.

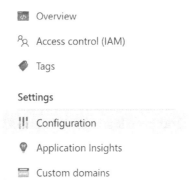

Figure 6-11. *Configuration Menu in Azure Portal*

3. Click the "+ Add" button, as seen in Figure 6-12.

Application settings   General settings

Application settings applicable to your site are encrypted at rest and transmitted over an encrypted channel. You can choose to display them in plain text in your browser by using the controls below. Learn more

Environment   Production

+ Add   ⊙ Show values   ✎ Advanced edit   🗑 Delete

▽ Filter application setting

☐   Name ↑   Value

No application setting to display

Figure 6-12. *Configuration Screen*

4. Give the configuration setting the same name as we used in the code, "CosmosDbConnectionString."

5. Paste the connection string from the value in the settings file into the value field.

6. Click OK.

The setting has been added, and we can see that the value for the setting is hidden unless we explicitly choose to see it.

Finally, we need to save the settings before we can use it.

7. Click "Save" on the configuration page, as seen in Figure 6-13.

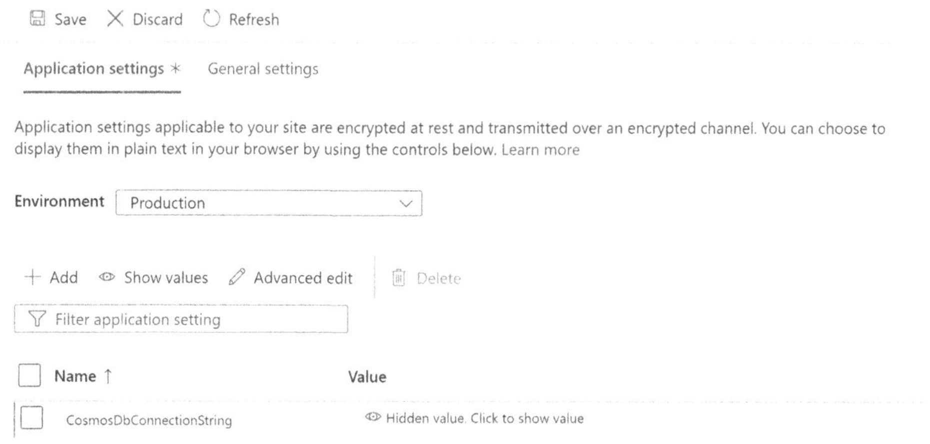

Figure 6-13. *Azure Static Web App Configuration Save*

Now that we have the setting in a safe place, our functions should work as expected. Let's rerun the production functions and see them working.

Great! We can now see the data from our database in production.

Conclusion

So, there we have it, our demo code from Part 1 has been removed, and we now have the basis for a real application! We've seen how to retrieve data from an Azure CosmosDB and return it using our Azure Function Api project.

Our application now has the ability to return a list of blog post summaries, as well as an individual blog post by id.

In the following chapter, we will see how to use this data in the front end to display it to the end user.

The source code for this book is available on GitHub, located at `https://github.com/Apress/beginning-azure-static-web-apps`. For this chapter, see the "chapter-6" folder.

CHAPTER 7

Displaying Data

In the previous chapter, we created our data source, seeded the data, and created two functions to retrieve both a list of blog post summaries and a single, complete blog post.

Now to make the front end of the site do something useful!

In this chapter, we will update the Client application to make HTTP requests to the Api to retrieve the summary list and individual blog posts. We'll then display those blog posts on the website using Razor components and even put our latest blog post on the index page so that it is one of the first things our visitors see when they arrive.

Technical Requirements

In order to complete the steps in this chapter, you will need to have the Azure Account created in Chapter 2, a deployed Azure Static Web App from Chapter 4, and the application from Chapter 6 available in a GitHub repository.

The source code for this book is available on GitHub, located at `https://github.com/Apress/beginning-azure-static-web-apps`. For this chapter, use the "chapter-6" folder for the start code.

Reading the Summaries

The first page that we are going to make will display the list of blog post summaries. To do this, we are going to create a service to retrieve the data from the API, a page for the user to land on, and a Blazor component to display the summary itself.

© Stacy Cashmore 2022
S. Cashmore, *Beginning Azure Static Web Apps*, https://doi.org/10.1007/978-1-4842-8146-8_7

Referencing the Models Project

To retrieve the objects from the API, we need to know what they look like. To do that, we need to add a reference to the Models project, as we did with the Api in the previous chapter.

1. In the Client project, right-click the "Dependencies" folder.

2. Click "Add Project Reference."

3. Ensure that "Models" is checked.

4. Click "OK."

Now that we have access to the BlogPost model, we can use it when retrieving data from the API.

Create the Service

Let's start with the service. This is going to use the HttpClient that we saw earlier in the FetchData page to communicate with the API and will also hold the data so that we only need to load the data once for each visit to the website.

1. Right-click the Client application and click "Add."

2. Click "New Folder."

3. Name the folder "Services."

4. Right-click the new "Services" folder and click "Add."

5. Click "Class."

6. In the window that opens (see Figure 7-1), name the class "BlogPostSummaryService."

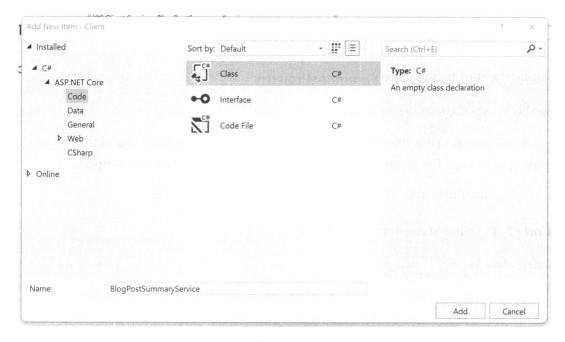

Figure 7-1. *New Class Dialog Window*

   7.   In the new class, we need to add a private HTTP Client and initialize it from the constructor.

Replace the contents of the new class with Code 7-1.

Code 7-1. BlogpostSummaryService Constructor

```csharp
namespace Client.Services;

public class BlogPostSummaryService
{
    private readonly HttpClient http;

    public BlogPostSummaryService(HttpClient http)
    {
        ArgumentNullException.ThrowIfNull(http, nameof(http));

        this.http = http;
    }
}
```

8. Add a public property, under the HTTP Client, to hold the blog
    post summaries that we retrieve; see Code 7-2.

Code 7-2. Public BlogPostSummary Property

```
public List<BlogPost>? Summaries;
```

As we are using the "BlogPost" from the Models project, we need to add the
namespace to this file to remove the red squiggly line from the last code snippet.

9. Add the using statement in Code 7-3 to the top of the file.

Code 7-3. Using Statement for Models

```
using Models;
```

If we look at the code, we see that the blog posts are not loaded in the constructor.
We are only going to load them when there is a need to. To provide access to that
functionality, we'll add a new method to the service.

10. Add the code from Code 7-4 underneath the constructor.

Code 7-4. LoadBlogPostSummaries Method

```
public async Task LoadBlogPostSummaries()
{
    if (Summaries == null)
    {
        Summaries = await http.GetFromJsonAsync➡
            <List<BlogPost>>("api/blogposts");
    }
}
```

We have another red squiggly line here; to use GetFromJsonAsync, we need to add
another using statement to the top of the file.

11. Add the using statement from Code 7-5 to the top of the file.

Code 7-5. Using Statement for System.Net.Http.Json

```
using System.Net.Http.Json;
```

The final thing we need to do for the service is to add it to our dependency injection container so that we can use it in our pages.

12. Open Program.cs and add the code snippet from Code 7-6 underneath where the HTTP Client is added to builder.services.

Code 7-6. Adding the BlogPostSummaryService to the builder.Services

```
builder.Services.AddScoped<BlogPostSummaryService>();
```

We also need to add the using statement so that the BlogPostSummaryService can be recognized.

13. Add the code from Code 7-7 to the top of the file.

Code 7-7. Using Statement for Client.Services

```
using Client.Services;
```

The service is now ready to use in our components. Let's create them!

Creating the Blog Post Summary Page

The first component that we are going to create is to display the list of blog posts.

1. To create the page, right-click the "Pages" folder in the "Client" app.

2. Click "Add."

3. Select "Razor Component..."; see Figure 7-2.

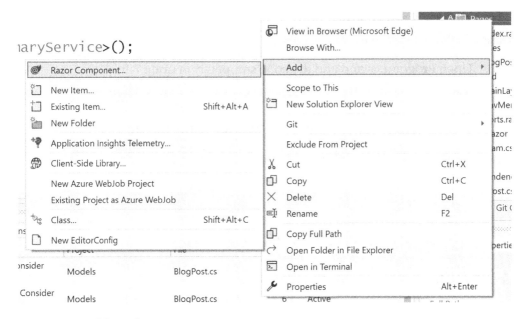

Figure 7-2. *Adding the Razor Component*

Depending on the version of Visual Studio 2022 that you have, you may also see the option to add a Razor Page – which seems the obvious choice when we are adding a page. However, these are not used for static Blazor applications. If you accidentally add one, you can simply delete it.

4. Give the Razor component the name "BlogPostSummaries.razor".

5. Remove the code in the file.

To turn our component into a page, we need to add an "@page" directive to the top. This directive will also tell the application what route to look for to load the page.

6. Add the directive from Code 7-8 to the top of the page.

Code 7-8. Page Directive

```
@page "/blogposts"
```

This component will now be loaded when we visit the "/blogposts" URL of our website.

7. Inject the BlogPostSummaryService into the page, as in Code 7-9.

Code 7-9. Injecting the BlogPostSummaryService

```
@inject BlogPostSummaryService service
```

We can see though that this causes a problem. The compiler doesn't know where to get the service from, so we get some red error highlighting on our code.

To fix that, we need to do one of two things. We can introduce a using statement in our page to tell the compiler where to look. This will work, but as we are going to be using this in multiple components, there is a better way.

In Blazor, there is a file that provides shared using statements for all Razor components. This is what we are going to change.

8. Open _Imports.razor from the root folder of the Client application.

9. At the end of the file, add the code from Code 7-10.

Code 7-10. Global Using Statement in _imports.razor

```
@using Client.Services
```

If we save the file and switch back to the "BlogPostSummaries.razor" page, we can see that the error highlighting is now gone.

Finally, we can start on the content of the page itself.

Firstly, we are going to make it easy for users to see where they are. We are going to change the page title in the browser tab and add a header to the page itself.

10. Add the code from Code 7-11.

Code 7-11. Page Title and Header

```
<PageTitle>Blog posts</PageTitle>

<h1>Blog posts</h1>
```

It looks like we have done the same thing twice here. Both the page title and the H1 have the same text. But they do different things. The page title is a built-in Blazor component that updates the title in the browser tab; the "h1" tag is to display the text on the page itself.

Now we need to get hold of our blog post summaries. For that, we are going to add a code block to our page. The great thing about Razor components is that they can do both markup and C# code. We could also use a code-behind file, where our code is in a separate file from the markup, but for code that we need on this page, that could be considered too much. However, it is a personal choice so pick whichever feels more natural.

This book does not cover the difference between code blocks and code-behind for Razor components. For more information, see `https://docs.microsoft.com/en-us/aspnet/core/blazor/components`.

11. Add the code from Code 7-12 at the end of the BlogPostSummaries.razor file.

Code 7-12. OnInitialized Code to Load BlogPostSummaries

```
@code
{
    protected override async Task OnInitializedAsync()
    {
        await service.LoadBlogPostSummaries();
    }
}
```

This function is called, as we can see from the name, when the page is initialized. It will fire off a call to the service to fetch the blog posts so that we can use them on the page.

While we are waiting for them though, we need to show our users information to let them know something is happening in the background.

12. Add the code from Code 7-13 after the h1 tags.

Code 7-13. Loading Information for Users

```
@if (service.Summaries is null)
{
    <div>Loading...</div>
}
```

Think back to our service. The list of blog post summaries is not set until we get the data from the API. So as long as it remains null, we know we are loading. When it has loaded, we will have a value for summaries, even if it is an empty list – so we can make a distinction between the two.

For now, we will just worry about showing the blog posts when they have loaded.

13.   Add the code from Code 7-14 underneath the code from Code 7-13.

Code 7-14.   Displaying the Titles of the Blog Posts

```
else
{
    foreach (var blogPostSummary in ➡
                    service.Summaries.OrderByDescending➡
                    (bps => bps.PublishedDate))
    {
        <div>@blogPostSummary.Title</div>
    }
}
```

This code will run through all the blog post summaries and put the title on the screen, newest first. Notice that we don't need to know when the blog post summary has a value; Blazor handles all of that automatically for us, so the loading text will disappear and be replaced with the titles.

Run the app, start the application in Visual Studio and then start the Static Web App CLI, and navigate to http://localhost:4280/blogposts to see the list of blog post titles.

Display the Whole Summary

That's a great start, but we want to show a bit more information than that and use it as a way to display the whole post.

Let's change the <div> for the code accordingly.

1.   Stop the application.

2.   Replace the code in the foreach loop with the code snippet from Code 7-15.

Code 7-15. BlogPost Summary Display Code

```
<article>
    <h2>@blogPostSummary.Title</h2>
    <div>
        @foreach(var tag in blogPostSummary.Tags)
        {
            <em>@tag, </em>
        }
    </div>
</article>
```

This will display everything except for the blog post itself. To do that, we need to convert the Markdown that we have for the blog post into HTML. This isn't something that we are going to make ourselves, we are going to use a well-known tool instead: Markdig.

You can find out more about Markdig on the GitHub repo, which can be found here: `https://github.com/xoofx/markdig`.

To use this tool, we are going to need to add a new NuGet package.

3. In the Client project, right-click "Dependencies."

4. Click "Manage NuGet Packages."

5. In the Browse tab, search for "Markdig.Signed".

6. Install the latest stable version.

Then we need to make the library available in our components. As we are going to be using it in multiple components, we'll add it in the _imports.razor as we did for the Client.Services.

7. Open the _imports.razor, and at the end of the file, add the code from Code 7-16.

Code 7-16. Global Using Statement for Markdig

```
@using Markdig
```

Now we have the code available to us, we just need to use it.

Back in BlogPostSummaries.razor, we are going to add one more line of markup to our blog post summary div.

8.   Under the Tags, add the code snippet from Code 7-17.

Code 7-17. Adding Blog Post Summary As HTML

```
<div>
    @((MarkupString)Markdown.ToHtml➦
        (blogPostSummary.BlogPostMarkdown))
</div>
```

This will take the Markdown that we are retrieving from the API and turn it into HTML to be displayed on the page.

Finally, for this page we need to add the link to the full blog post! We are going to make the whole article tag clickable for ease of use.

To do this, we are going to change the opening article tag in the foreach loop.

9.   Replace the opening "article" tag with the code snippet from Code 7-18.

Code 7-18. Making the Opening Div Clickable

```
<article @onclick="() => Navigate(blogPostSummary.Id, ➦
    blogPostSummary.Author)">
```

Whenever the div is clicked, we will call the Navigate command. Let's add that next.

10.   Inside of our code block, we need to add the code from Code 7-19.

Code 7-19. Navigate Function

```
void Navigate(Guid id, string author) => ➦
    navigationManager.NavigateTo➦
    ($"/blogposts/{author}/{id}");
```

The NavigationManager is an injectable object that helps us navigate to different pages inside of our Blazor application. As it's injectable, we need to inject it.

11. Add the line from Code 7-20 underneath the @page directive at the top of the page.

Code 7-20. Injecting the NavigationManager

```
@inject NavigationManager navigationManager
```

Our page is now complete. The only thing left now is to add an easy way to navigate to the page. We are going to add a navigation option in the sidebar of our application for this.

12. In the "Shared" folder of the Client project, open the "NavMenu. razor" file.

13. Add the code snippet from Code 7-21 underneath the home NavLink.

Code 7-21. NavLink for the Blog Post Page

```
<div class="nav-item px-3">
    <NavLink class="nav-link" href="blogposts">
        <span class="oi oi-document" aria-hidden="true">➡
                </span> Blog Posts
    </NavLink>
</div>
```

This will add a new navigation link for our page, with the text Blog Posts and a document icon on the button.

Now we can run the application and test that the navigation works as expected and that the summaries are displayed. If we click the blog post summary itself, we land on a page that doesn't yet exist. This is where our full blog post is going to be displayed. Let's add that now!

Displaying the Whole Blog Post

As with the blog post summaries, we are going to add the full blog post in two steps: a new service, which is slightly different to the one that we just made, and a new page to display the blog post.

Reading the Blog Post

To get the full blog post, we are going to add a new service, but this one is going to behave a little differently.

We are not going to read every full blog post in one go. But we are also not going to fetch the blog post every time we want to display it. We are going to have a local store of blog posts; when a request comes in, we'll check to see if we already have it available and return it from the cache.

This will help make the application more performant when revisiting blog post that we have already opened and reduce unnecessary calls to the API.

Should we not have the post in cache, we'll make a call to the API to fetch the blog post and store it for future use.

1. In the "Client" project, in the "Services" folder, make a new class called "BlogPostService.cs".

As we did with the "BlogPostSummaryService," we need to add a private HTTP Client and initialize it from the constructor.

2. Replace the existing code with the code snippet from Code 7-22.

Code 7-22. BlogpostService Constructor

```
using Microsoft.AspNetCore.Components;
using System.Net.Http.Json;
using Models;

namespace Client.Services;

public class BlogPostService
{
    private readonly HttpClient http;
    private readonly NavigationManager navigationManager;

    public BlogPostService(
        HttpClient http,
        NavigationManager navigationManager)
    {
        ArgumentNullException.ThrowIfNull(http, nameof(http));
        ArgumentNullException.ThrowIfNull(
```

```
        navigationManager,
        nameof(navigationManager));

    this.http = http;
    this.navigationManager = navigationManager;
  }
}
```

3.   Add the variable to hold our blog posts as in Code 7-23.

Code 7-23.   List for Holding Blog Posts

```
private List<BlogPost> blogPostCache = new();
```

Now we can add the code that is going to fetch the blog posts for us.

4.   Add the code from Code 7-24 before the final "}" in the file.

Code 7-24.   GetBlogPost Function

```
public async Task<BlogPost?> GetBlogPost(➡
      Guid blogPostId, string author)
{
      BlogPost? blogPost = blogPostCache.FirstOrDefault➡
          (bp => bp.Id == blogPostId && bp.Author == author);

      if (blogPost is null)
      {
          var result = await http.GetAsync➡
              ($"api/blogposts/{author}/{blogPostId}");
          if (!result.IsSuccessStatusCode)
          {
              navigationManager.NavigateTo("404");
              return null;
          }

          blogPost = await➡
              result.Content.ReadFromJsonAsync<BlogPost>();

          if (blogPost is null)
```

```
        {
            navigationManager.NavigateTo("404");
            return null;
        }

        blogPostCache.Add(blogPost);
    }

    return blogPost;
}
```

This function first checks to see if there is a blog post in our cache with the Id and author that we are looking for. If it is not found, we try to retrieve it from the API.

If we get an HTTP 404 or null response from the API, we know we are trying to access a blog post that doesn't exist and should redirect to page 404.

This page doesn't exist, and so the Blazor router will display our content not found information. There are better ways of doing this inside of Blazor, but they fall outside the scope of this book.

If we get a blog post back from the API, then we store it in the blogPostCache.

Finally, we return the blog post to the caller.

That is our second service finished.

5.   Add it to the builder.Services in the "Program.cs" file, as per Code 7-25.

Code 7-25. Adding the BlogPostService to the builder.Services

```
builder.Services.AddScoped<BlogPostService>();
```

Now that our BlogPostService is available, let's put the actual blog post on the screen.

Display Blog Post

We have our blog post so we can make the page display it!

1.   Add a new razor component in the "Pages" folder called "FullBlogPost.razor".

2.   As with the page for the blog post summaries, remove all the code in the page and start from scratch.

3. Add the @page directive from Code 7-26 to the top of the page.

Code 7-26. Page Directive for the Blog Post Page

```
@page "/blogposts/{author}/{id:guid}"
```

This makes our page available on the same URL as the summaries, with the id and author of the blog post being added to differentiate it. This also makes the id and author available to us in the code – we'll get to that shortly.

Before that, we are going to inject our new service so that we can retrieve the blog posts.

4. Add the code from Code 7-27 under the @page directive.

Code 7-27. Injecting the BlogPostService

```
@inject BlogPostService service
```

Now we can add the code to fetch the blog post. Whereas for the summaries we accessed the list of summaries directly from the service, for the blog post we are going to make a private variable for the blog post directly on the page.

We also check that the parameter we have is the correct one.

5. Add the code snippet from Code 7-28 under the @inject statement from Code 7-27.

Code 7-28. Fetching the Blog Post

```
@using Models

@code
{
    private BlogPost? blogPost;

    [Parameter]
    public Guid Id { get; set; }

    [Parameter]
    public string Author { get; set; }

    protected override async Task OnParametersSetAsync()
```

```
    {
         blogPost = await service.GetBlogPost(Id, Author);
    }
}
```

Now that we have the blog post, we can display it on the screen.
For this, we are going to be using similar code as for the summary.

6. Add the code from Code 7-29 above "@code".

Code 7-29. Display the Blog Post

```
@if (blogPost is null)
{
    <div>Loading...</div>
}
else
{
        <article>
                <h1>@blogPost.Title</h1>
                <h2>@blogPost.Author</h2>
                <div>@blogPost.PublishedDate</div>
                <div>
                        @foreach(var tag in blogPost.Tags)
                        {
                              <em>@tag, </em>
                        }
                </div>
                <div>
                        @((MarkupString)Markdown.ToHtml⮕
                              (blogPost.BlogPostMarkdown))
                </div>
        </article>
}
```

While the blog post is being loaded, we display the "Loading..." page. Once we have it, we display the post as we intended.

Add the First Blog Post to the Index Page

Finally, we are going to add our blog post to one more location. When people first come to the site, it would be good to let them see the latest blog post that we have published.

To do that, we are going to take the div that displays our blog post summary and turn it into a reusable component. Then we are going to get the blog post summaries on the index page and display just the latest one.

Prepare the Index.razor File

The first thing that we need to do is inject the BlogPostSummaryService into the index page and add a using statement so that we can access the blog post itself.

1. In the Client project, in the Pages folder, open the "index. razor" page.

2. Add the code from the code snippet in Code 7-30 under the @page directive.

Code 7-30. Inject and Using Statements for Index.razor

```
@inject BlogPostSummaryService service
@using Models
```

To get the blog post summary, we need a couple of functions: one to load the summaries if needed and one to fetch the latest summary.

3. Add the code from Code 7-31 at the end of the file.

Code 7-31. Index.razor Code for Loading Summaries and Selecting the Latest

```
@code {
    private BlogPost? Summary =>
            service.Summaries?
            .OrderByDescending(bps => bps.PublishedDate)
            .FirstOrDefault();
```

```
protected override async Task OnInitializedAsync()
{
    await service.LoadBlogPostSummaries();
}
}
```

The load summaries in the OnInitializedAsync are the same as we have used before.

The Summary property is what we will be using in our code. It takes all the summaries from the service, orders them by their published date in descending order and then takes the first one.

Next, we are going to add code to display the loading message, a message for when we have no blog posts, and finally to display the blog post summary itself.

4. Add the code from Code 7-32 above the @code directive.

Code 7-32. Displaying the Latest Blog Post

```
@if (service.Summaries == null)
{
    <div>Loading…</div>
}
else
{
    <div>
        <h2>Recent Blog Post</h2>
        @if (Summary == null)
        {
            <p class="byline">No blog posts found 😵</p>
        }
        else
        {
            <div class="home-page">
                <BlogPostSummary Summary="@Summary" />
            </div>
        }
    </div>
}
```

Right now, the BlogPostSummary HTML tag doesn't exist. This will be a new razor component that we will use both here and in our blog post summary page.

Create the BlogPostSummary Component

We are going to group our components together, the same as we have done for our services.

1. In the Client project, add a new folder called "Components."

2. Add a new Razor component in this folder and call it "BlogPostSummary."

   The naming is very important here as it determines the tag that we will add to our code.

The code for the component is very similar to the blog post summary page, with a couple of small adjustments.

3. Replace the contents of the newly created component with the code snippet from Code 7-33.

Code 7-33. BlogPostSummary Component Markup

```
@using Models
@inject NavigationManager navigationManager

<article @onclick=@Navigate>
    <h2>@Summary.Title</h2>
    <div>
        @foreach(var tag in Summary.Tags)
        {
            <em>@tag, </em>
        }
    </div>
    <div>
            @((MarkupString)Markdown.ToHtml➡
                (Summary.BlogPostMarkdown))
    </div>
</article>
```

```
@code{
    [Parameter]
    public BlogPost Summary { get; set; }

    void Navigate() => navigationManager➥
            .NavigateTo($"/blogposts/{Summary.Author}➥
            /{Summary.Id}");
}
```

For the component, there is no @page directive at the top. That is what marks the difference between a component and a page in Blazor.

A page is a component and can be used as such. But a component without the directive cannot be used as a page.

At the end of the file, we have a small @code block. This defines the parameter that is used to pass the BlogPost into the component and also replicates the Navigate method needed to go to the blog post page. This is a little simpler than in the BlogPostSummaries page as we no longer need to pass through the id and author of the BlogPost to the Navigate function. We can just use the data directly from the BlogPost passed in the parameter.

Before we add the code to the blog post summary and index pages, we need to add the namespace to the "_imports.razor" file so that the component can be used. There is just one problem – nowhere in this file do we say what the namespace is.

Thankfully, it's easy to work out. The namespace for components is taken from the folder structure where the component is located. As we called our folder "Components," and it is in the "Client" project, our namespace will be "Client.Components".

4. Open the _imports.razor and add the code from Code 7-34 to the end of the file.

Code 7-34. Global Using for Client.Components

```
@using Client.Components
```

Our component is now ready for use!

Change the Blog Post Summary Page

Seeing as we have added a component for the blog post that replicates the functionality we already have on our blog post summary page, we are going to simplify the page by using this component here as well.

1. Open the BlogPostSummaries.razor page.

2. Replace all the code inside of the foreach loop with the code from Code 7-35.

Code 7-35. Code for Using BlogPostSummary Component

```
<BlogPostSummary Summary="@blogPostSummary" />
```

3. Remove the Navigate function and the associated @inject statement for the NavigationManager.

   This functionality is now handled in the BlogPostSummary component.

The final file should look like Code 7-36.

Code 7-36. Final BlogPostSummaries.razor File

```
@page "/blogposts"
@inject BlogPostSummaryService service

<PageTitle>Blog posts</PageTitle>

<h1>Blog posts</h1>

@if (service.BlogPostSummaries is null)
{
    <div>Loading...</div>
}
else
{
        foreach (var blogPostSummary in ➡
            service.Summaries.OrderByDescending➡
            (bps => bps.PublishedDate))
        {
```

```
        <BlogPostSummary Summary="@ blogPostSummary" />
    }
}

@code
{
    protected override void OnInitializedAsync()
    {
        await service.LoadBlogPostSummaries();
    }
}
```

Our website is now ready to run!

Checking Our Results

We have an application that should now display useful information to us. Let's check it both locally and in production.

Running Locally

Before we push to GitHub, and so to our production environment, let's run this locally to check that it's working.

Start the application in Visual Studio, and then run the Static Web App CLI.

On the first page, you should see a page similar to Figure 7-3.

Figure 7-3. *Index Page with Latest Blog Post Summary*

If we go to the blog post page in the navigation, we should see a list of blog posts, as in Figure 7-4.

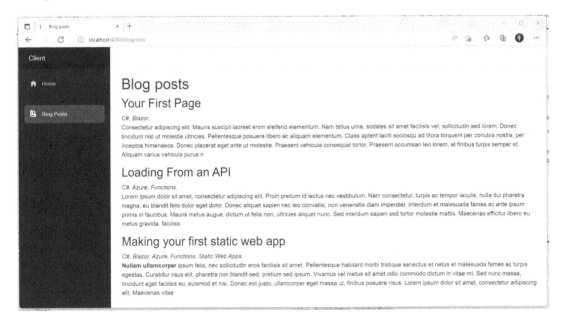

Figure 7-4. *List of Blog Post Summaries*

And finally, if we open one of the blog posts, we should see the full post, as in Figure 7-5.

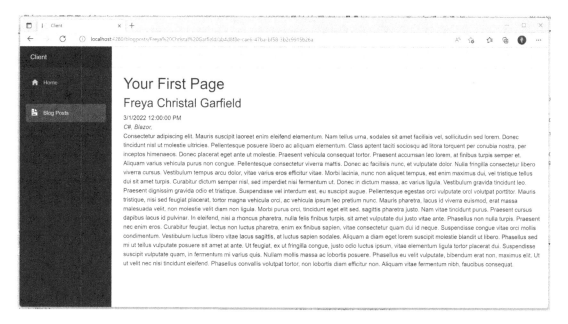

Figure 7-5. *Full Blog Post*

Deploy Blog Post

As our code is working locally, we can now push it to production. Go to the git window in Visual Studio, add a commit message – e.g., Added Blog Posts – and commit and push to production.

If we check the GitHub actions for our repository, we should see that the site is rebuilding and deploying.

Once this has finished, open the website in a browser and check that the site looks the same as it does locally.

We do have one problem remaining that we need to solve for our users. From the index page, click the blog post summary to open the full blog post. Now refresh the page.

Problem… We have a page not found error (see Figure 7-6) that we still need to take care of. We'll look into how to solve that in the next chapter.

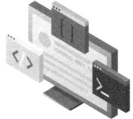

Figure 7-6. *Azure Static Web Apps 404 Error Page*

Conclusion

For the first time, we now have a website that does something useful!

When visitors visit our site, they will see the latest blog post, a page with summaries of all the blog posts, and a page for the blog post itself.

There are still problems that we need to solve though, for example, ensuring that we can refresh the page or deep link directly to the blog post.

In the next chapter, we'll fix these problems and take a deeper look at the way that we can control the Azure Static Web App from code using the staticwebapp.config.json configuration file.

The source code for this book is available on GitHub, located at `https://github.com/Apress/beginning-azure-static-web-apps`. For this chapter, use the "chapter-7" folder.

CHAPTER 8

Static Web App Configuration

We did it! At the end of the last chapter, we have an application that we could deploy and let our users see the content that we are creating. Sure, we need to style it to suit our personal tastes, but all our content is there.

But we still have a problem with making it nice to use. One big problem is that when users refresh their page anywhere except for the index, they get a 404 error. Not wonderful.

This also gives us a different usability problem. No one can deep link or share our content. No one wants to share the index page and tell people how to access the content. They want to share a deep link to the content itself.

Thankfully, we can solve that – and do much more – using the Static Web App Configuration file. That is going to be our focus in this chapter.

Technical Requirements

To complete the steps in this chapter, you will need to have the Azure Account created in Chapter 2, a deployed Azure Static Web App from Chapter 4, and the application from Chapter 7 available in a GitHub repository.

The source code for this book is available on GitHub, located at `https://github.com/Apress/beginning-azure-static-web-apps`. For this chapter, use the "chapter-7" folder for the start code.

© Stacy Cashmore 2022
S. Cashmore, *Beginning Azure Static Web Apps*, https://doi.org/10.1007/978-1-4842-8146-8_8

Creating the staticwebapp.config.json File

The first thing that we want to do is create the file that will be used when we deploy to Azure.

If we look at our code again, and specifically the Client project, we can see a folder called "wwwroot." This is a special folder in a Blazor project that is copied to the application when published. Its contents are copied unaltered. You can see the location in Figure 8-1.

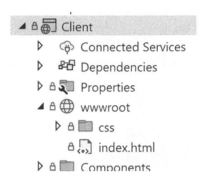

Figure 8-1. *wwwroot Folder in the Client Project*

So, this is where we are going to store our staticwebapp.config.json file.

1. Right-click the wwwroot folder.

2. Click Add.

3. Click "New Item."

4. In the search box, look for "json."

5. Select JSON File.

6. Name the file "staticwebapp.config.json" as in Figure 8-2.

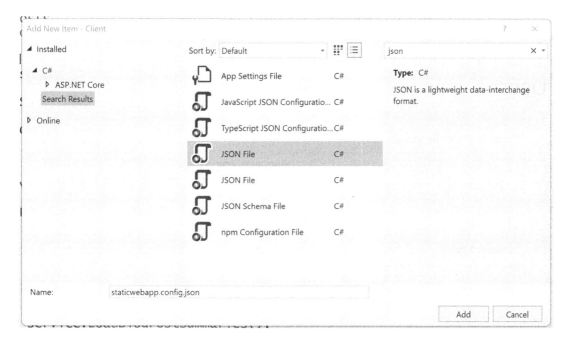

Figure 8-2. *Add staticwebapp.config.json*

Now that we have a file, we can start by fixing the issue with refreshing the page!

Navigation Fallback

The problem that we have with refreshing our blog post page or sharing a link that goes directly to the page rather than via the menu is that the page itself doesn't exist in our published website.

Traditionally when a browser loads a page, it goes to the server, requests a page, downloads the contents, and displays it. When we navigate to a different page, there is another request to the server for that page, and we download that page as well, as described by Figure 8-3.

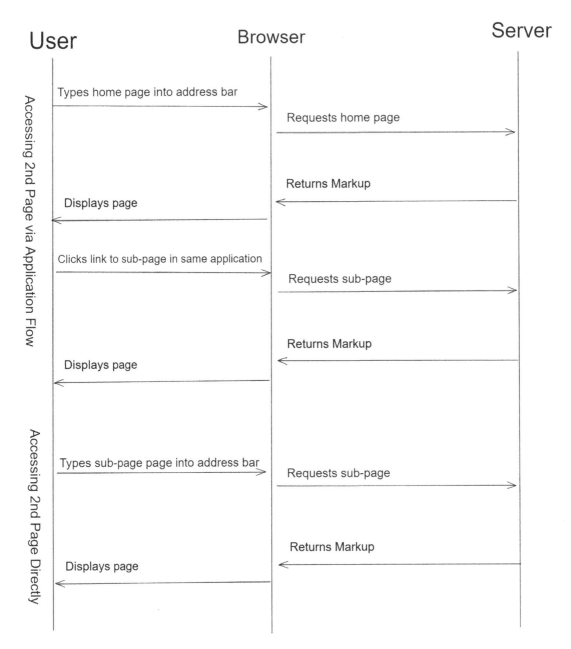

Figure 8-3. *Simplified Page Request Flow for Server Side Generated Applications*

A Single Page Application (SPA), such as our Blazor application, doesn't work in this way though.

That first request to the server doesn't deliver a page; rather, it delivers application code that runs inside the browser. The browser then builds the page itself.

When the navigation to the second page is received, the SPA builds this new page without needing to make the round trip to the server.

However, if we try to call that second page directly, the SPA isn't loaded and so the browser does make that round trip to the server. Only the page isn't a file on the server and so we can't find it.

It **only** exists inside of the SPA application itself – and so we get a 404, file not found, error when trying to call it directly, as described by Figure 8-4.

Single Page Application (SPA)

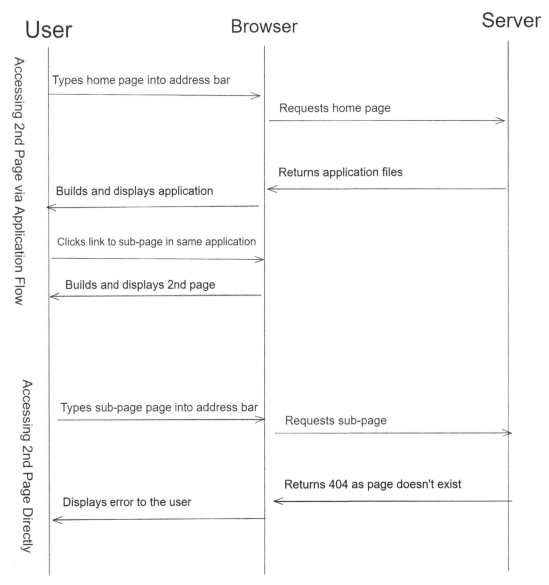

Figure 8-4. *Simplified Page Request Flow for Single Page Applications*

By using the navigation fallback though, we can control what happens when a path isn't found on the server. We are going to use the index.html as our navigation fallback. So, when a request is sent to the Azure Static Web App for a route that doesn't exist, it will use the index.html for the contents.

This will load our application and ensure that the correct route for the URL is loaded (or display the contents of the not found route).

1. Open the staticwebapp.config.json file we just created.

2. Replace the contents with the code from Code 8-1.

Code 8-1. Navigation Fallback in the staticwebapp.config.json File

```
{
  "navigationFallback": {
    "rewrite": "index.html",
    "exclude": [
      "/images/*.{png,jpg,gif}",
      "/css/*",
      "/api/*"
    ]
  }
}
```

As stated, this code will use the contents of the index.html page for any route that isn't known so that Blazor can then route the application to the correct page on the client.

However, we also exclude a few routes from this. Images, CSS files, and API calls are a special case. For these, we do not want to load the index.html and let Blazor try to construct a page. Rather, we want to return the standard 404 response.

Before we move on to the other options that we have, let's deploy the file so that our site can redeploy with the fallback in place.

Commit the changes in the git changes window inside of Visual Studio, and push. Once the deploy has finished, you can navigate back to one of the blog posts and refresh the page to see our changes working.

Routes

To control resources in our application, we have the "routes" property in the staticwebapp.config.json file. This property is an array of "route" rules. These control rewriting and redirecting resources (along with the HTTP status code for the response), role-based access control (RBAC) to those resources, and custom control of the response headers – both adding and removing headers.

The properties available for this control are displayed in Table 8-1.

Table 8-1. *Route Object Properties*

Property	Notes	Description
route	Required	The route to be matched, this may include a wildcard at the end of the path to match all subroutes
methods		This property allows the route matching to be more fine-tuned – not only on the route itself but also the HTTP method used for access
redirect	Mutually exclusive with rewrite	Points from the selected resource to a different place. The user sees the change in their browser. By default, this is a 302 (temporary redirect) response code, but can be overwritten to be a 301 (permanent redirect)
rewrite	Mutually exclusive with redirect	Returns a resource from a different location without updating the user's browser location
statusCode		This can be used to override the status code returned or the request
headers		A set of HTTP headers added to the response. These can add to, override, or remove one or more of the global headers from the website. To remove a header, the value is set to an empty string in the array
allowedRoles		Used in role-based access to identify who can access a resource

We are going to concentrate on using these to manage three scenarios:

- Restricting access to our API for specific users

- Blocking access to certain resources

- Handling resources that have moved, both temporarily and permanently

Restricting Access to Resources

The following configuration snippets/example staticwebapp.config.json are for illustration purposes only. We are not going to add them to our project.

To start, we are going to see how to remove access to certain resources. There may be reasons why you do not want people to access some resources on your web application. This can especially be the case for those built-in Azure Static Web App resources that we do not have control over in our website (we will cover some of these resources in the next chapter). These resources are always available, as they come from the Azure Static Web App itself. But we can ensure that our users can't access them.

Let's assume that we do not want people to use any of the authentication that is built into Azure Static Web Apps. We can add the json code from Code 8-2 to control that.

Code 8-2. Restrict Access to the Azure Static Web App Authentication Resources

```
"routes": [
  {
    "route": "/.auth/*",
    "statusCode": 404
  }
],
```

This snippet will set the routes array to contain a single route, which will match against all resources under the path "./auth" and return a 404 response. While the resources will still exist in our Azure Static Web App, we cannot control that; it will mean that they can no longer be accessed.

Protecting Resources

In the last section, we stopped access to a resource completely. However, there are times when we don't want to stop access for everyone, but do want to make sure that only certain people can access our resources.

Next, we are going to make a resource only available to users with a specific role.

We are not going into how to assign the role needed to gain access yet – that is going to be covered in the following chapter.

Some resources, whether that is an API call or static file, should only be available to certain users. Either only users that are authenticated on our site or maybe a subset of those users.

The snippet from Code 8-3 specifies a `routes` json array with a single route that would restrict all resources under the path "/protected" for users that are authenticated. Those not authenticated would instead get a 401 not authorized response.

Code 8-3. Restrict /protected Resources to Authenticated Users

```
"routes": [
  {
    "route": "/protected/*",
    "allowedRoles": ["authenticated"]
  }
]
```

We can also restrict access based on the HTTP method being used for a route. For example, you can let one group of users access a resource to "get" data for read-only access, not allowing them to "post" or "put" data to write data back. In the example from Code 8-4, we allow all users to read data, but only authenticated users to write.

Code 8-4. Restrict Access to an API for Write Access

```
"routes": [
    {
        "route": "/api/readwriteapi",
        "methods": ["POST", "PUT", "PATCH", "DELETE"],
        "allowedRoles": ["authenticated"]
    }
]
```

This will allow all "safe" HTTP methods that should not change data (GET, HEAD, and OPTIONS) to "/api/readwriteapi" but will deny access to the methods that can change the state of the server unless the user is authenticated.

While we can also restrict direct access to pages in our Client application using these routes, there is more work needed to make the application secure. This will be covered in the next chapter.

Moving Resources – Temporarily

There are times when you need to move a resource for a short period of time. When doing this, you don't want to impact how findable your page is, because it will be moving back again. For this, we can use the 302 redirect. This will redirect to the new page but let whoever has requested the page know that the move is not permanent. An example of this can be seen in Code 8-5.

Code 8-5. Redirecting Temporarily Using a 302 Redirect

```
"routes": [
        {
            "route": "/resource",
            "redirect": "/temporaryresource",
            "statusCode": 302
        }
]
```

This snippet will redirect all calls to "/resource" to "/temporaryresource" with a 302 response so that "/resource" does not lose its SEO significance.

Moving Resources – Permanently

Sometimes, we will move an object permanently – for example, should we change the structure of the site or change the name of a folder. In such cases, we still want external links to work, but we don't want the same page to be available in multiple places for search engines. In Code 8-6, we can see an example of this.

Code 8-6. Redirecting Permanently Using a 302 Redirect

```
"routes": [
    {
        "route": "/oldresource",
        "redirect": "/newresource",
        "statusCode": 301
    }
]
```

This looks almost the same as Code 8-5, except for the code used for the redirect. This code informs the requester that the resource has been moved permanently and will not return to the original location. This should not be used for temporary redirects as it can cause permanent changes to the SEO of the original location.

Response Overrides

When something goes wrong with a request, an error code is returned. To improve the user experience, and to keep the design of our application consistent, we can override the error responses with our own custom pages, as shown in Code 8-7.

Code 8-7. Response Override Setting for Forbidden 403

```
"responseOverrides": {
  "403": {
    "rewrite": "/forbidden.html"
  }
}
```

Using this snippet, the user will see our custom page rather than the standard forbidden page of the Azure Static Web App if they do not have the correct rights to access that resource.

Example Configuration

We've looked at some of the components available individually; now let's look at an example with all the options we've used, as seen in Code 8-8.

Code 8-8. Example of a Complete staticwebapp.config.json

```
{
  "routes": [
    {
      "route": "/protected/*",
      "allowedRoles": [ "authenticated" ]
    },
```

```
    {
      "route": "/api/readwriteapi",
      "methods": [ "POST", "PUT", "PATCH", "DELETE" ],
      "allowedRoles": [ "authenticated" ]
    },
    {
      "route": "/oldresource",
      "redirect": "/newresource",
      "statusCode": 301
    },
    {
      "route": "/resource",
      "redirect": "/temporaryresource",
      "statusCode": 302
    },
    {
      "route": "/.auth/*",
      "statusCode": 404
    }
  ],
  "navigationFallback": {
    "rewrite": "index.html",
    "exclude": [
      "/images/*.{png,jpg,gif}",
      "/css/*",
      "/api/*"
    ]
  },
  "responseOverrides": {
    "403": {
      "rewrite": "/forbidden.html"
    }
  }
}
```

We will be using these settings in the upcoming chapters to complete the base of our blog application. Except for the redirect/rewrite functionality, which is just useful to know as your application evolves.

Conclusion

The Static Web App Configuration provides us with control over our deployed application. Not only for the simple things that we should always remember to implement, navigationFallback, for example, to make our site more usable but also deeper control of the application.

We've touched upon the configuration for functionality that we'll be using in upcoming chapters and some good-to-know settings. The staticwebapp.config.json file is capable of much more though! For both the basic free tier version and the more advanced standard tier. The full documentation for all options can be found at `https://docs.microsoft.com/en-us/azure/static-web-apps/configuration`.

In the coming chapter, we'll use these settings to work on the part of the application that we will be using more than our blog post readers: creating and editing posts. In fact, not more than our blog post readers – our blog post readers should not have access to blog post creation and editing functionality at all!

That's why we'll begin with looking at the built-in authentication providers and ensure that we can log in to our application and be assigned a role that means only authorized users can edit the content.

The source code for this book is available on GitHub, located at `https://github.com/Apress/beginning-azure-static-web-apps`. For this chapter, see the "chapter-8" folder.

PART III

Authentication

In the previous part, we created an application that allowed users to read blog posts that we have written.

That's a great start, but to make it really useful, we want to be able to manage those blog posts as well.

In this part, we will be looking at authentication in Azure Static Web Apps, making it possible for users to authenticate, adding role-based access to ensure that only people with the correct rights can manage data, and looking at the limitations of the free tier with regard to authentication.

Once we have authentication in our application, we will add the management functionality itself. By the end, we will have an application where we can safely and securely manage the data in our application.

CHAPTER 9

Authentication

Up until now, we have been working anonymously in our application. To read blog posts, we do not need to know who the user is – our blog post will be open to all for reading.

However, now we want to allow only certain users to be able to add new blog posts or edit existing ones. To do this, we need authentication and authorization.

Authentication to know who is using our application, and authorization to know what roles that user has, and what they should be allowed to do within the application.

In this chapter, we are going to be looking at the authentication options available inside of Azure Static Web Apps for the free tier and how to add role-based authorization to those users.

Finally, we will add the code needed to use this functionality in both our Client and Api projects to secure our application.

Technical Requirements

To complete the steps in this chapter, you will need to have the Azure Account created in Chapter 2, a deployed Azure Static Web App from Chapter 4, and the application from Chapter 8 available in a GitHub repository.

The source code for this book is available on GitHub, located at `https://github.com/Apress/beginning-azure-static-web-apps`. For this chapter, use the "chapter-8" folder for the start code.

Authentication Basics

The best way to manage your users' passwords is to never know them in the first place. But we still need to allow users to log in to our application. So how can we do that if we do not know their passwords?

© Stacy Cashmore 2022
S. Cashmore, *Beginning Azure Static Web Apps*, https://doi.org/10.1007/978-1-4842-8146-8_9

We've discussed the extras that we get with Azure Static Web Apps – the glue that joins the static files and API to make one coherent application etc. Authentication and authorization are another part of this, designed to make our lives simpler.

The Azure Static Web App integrates to several platforms, allowing us to use social logins for our application without having to set up the connection ourselves. We let those platforms deal with the users' login information so that we don't need to worry about it ourselves.

Using this built-in authentication doesn't only make it simpler for us to add authentication, and help keep passwords safer, but it also means that we don't have to add code to our application to implement the actual authentication – only to make use of it. That means less possibility for us to introduce bugs!

Standard Authentication

In the Azure Static Web App free tier that we are using for our application, we have access to the standard authentication features.

At the time of writing, we have three authentication providers available to us, with one more in preview (but usable). See Table 9-1 for details.

Table 9-1. *Azure Static Web App Authentication Providers*

Provider	Notes	URL
Azure Active Directory	Used for Microsoft accounts	aad
Twitter		twitter
GitHub		github
Google	In preview at the time of writing	google

After using Azure Static Web Apps since they were in preview, the ability to use these login providers out of the box is still one of the features that I find most amazing.

They are also implemented in such a way that our application doesn't need to know, for the most part, what provider we are using. The integration for our application remains the same no matter which authentication provider the user chooses. And should we upgrade to a standard tier Azure Static Web App in the future, it will still work without changes.

To see this in action, let's try this out on our production application. We don't have any code written to implement authentication, but we can access the built-in functions via the URL.

All Azure Static Web App authentication functions are available via the "./auth" path of our application. Each provider has their own endpoint within this route.

The login pages are located behind "./auth/login/<provider>", where "<provider>" is "aad," "twitter," "github," or "google."

1. Visit the login page of your website.
   In the example from Code 9-1, twitter is used; you can, however, use your preferred provider using the URL column from Table 9-1.

Code 9-1. Twitter Login Page Link

```
http://<your website domain>/.auth/login/twitter
```

We see that the web application redirects to the provider of choice and goes through the authentication process of the provider, before displaying the consent page for the user.

This is needed because the provider will pass some user details through to the Azure Static Web App. An example can be seen in Figure 9-1.

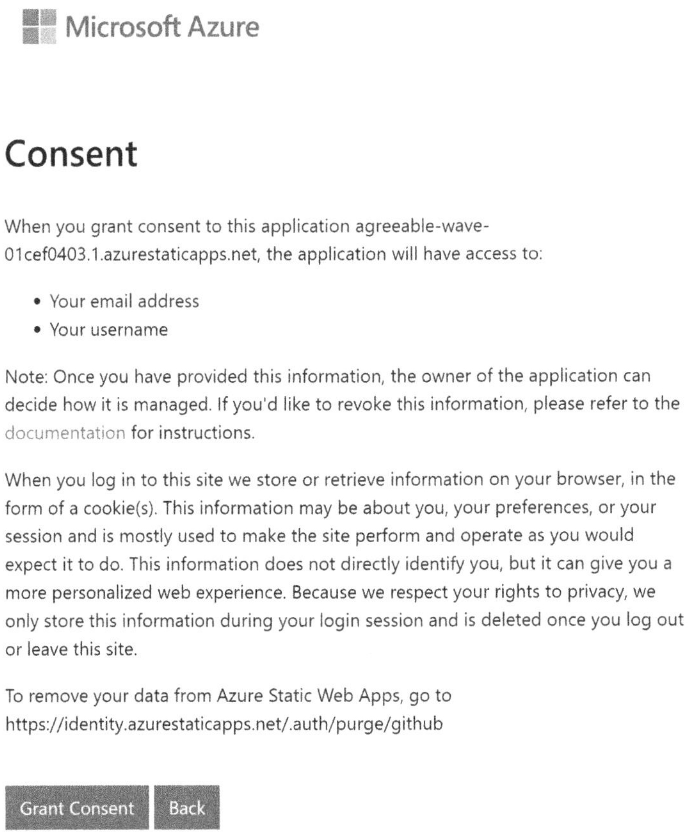

Consent

When you grant consent to this application agreeable-wave-01cef0403.1.azurestaticapps.net, the application will have access to:

- Your email address
- Your username

Note: Once you have provided this information, the owner of the application can decide how it is managed. If you'd like to revoke this information, please refer to the documentation for instructions.

When you log in to this site we store or retrieve information on your browser, in the form of a cookie(s). This information may be about you, your preferences, or your session and is mostly used to make the site perform and operate as you would expect it to do. This information does not directly identify you, but it can give you a more personalized web experience. Because we respect your rights to privacy, we only store this information during your login session and is deleted once you log out or leave this site.

To remove your data from Azure Static Web Apps, go to https://identity.azurestaticapps.net/.auth/purge/github

Grant Consent   Back

Figure 9-1. *Consent Screen for Azure Static Web App Authentication*

Once consent has been given, we return to the application again. This consent request only happens the first time a user authenticates with a provider for this Azure Static Web App.

As we do not have any code to use this authentication information, we do not see anything in the site to let us know that we have authenticated. But there is a page that can display the information to us.

ClientPrincipal

We don't only have the login pages available to use; there are also resources for us to see the currently authenticated user.

1. Navigate to the "/.auth/me" page of your deployed application.

When authenticated, this resource returns a JSON object containing information about our user; see Code 9-2 for an example.

Code 9-2. Example ClientPrincipal from the "./auth/me" Resource

```
{
  "clientPrincipal": {
    "identityProvider": "twitter",
    "userId": "8d29475abc694fe69f7db06d4edcc234",
    "userDetails": "Stacy_Cash",
    "userRoles": [
      "anonymous",
      "authenticated"
    ]
  }
}
```

Let's take a short look at the information that we have available to us in this object.

identityProvider

The provider used to authenticate the user. For standard authentication, "aad," "twitter," "github," or "google."

userId

When a user logs in to an Azure Static Web App using standard authentication, a user id is generated for them. This Id is unique for the user, so we can use it to identify users when they use our application.

This Id is also unique to this one Azure Static Web App. If we have multiple applications, then the same user will have a different userId in each one.

userDetails

This is the identity of the user passed through from the authentication provider. What is returned depends on the provider used. For "aad" and "google," we receive the email of the authenticated user. For "twitter" and "github," we receive the user handle.

userRoles

Finally, we have an array of roles associated with our authenticated user. The two roles that we can see in Code 9-2 are the default roles that every authenticated user is assigned when they log in to an Azure Static Web app. We do not need to add these roles ourselves.

Accessing Authentication Data in Our Application

Because the browser includes the authentication token set by the Azure Static Web App when requests are made to the resource, we see the correct data for the authenticated user here. And because our Client application is a Single Page Application that runs inside of the browser, we can call this resource from our application to use for authentication and authorization purposes. We'll cover that later in this chapter.

For our API, we authenticate in a slightly different way. The API runs inside of the Azure Static Web App itself and so cannot call the "./auth/me" endpoint with the authentication cookie.

Thankfully, the authentication glue that provides that resource also solves the problem for us. When a request passes from the Client app through the Azure Static Web App to our Azure Function, an extra HTTP header is added to the application: `x-ms-client-principal`. This contains a Base64 string encoded version of the same ClientPrincipal that we have available to us in the Client. Because this header is not sent via the Client application but added by the Azure Static Web App itself, the data included is trustworthy.

Using these resources, we can add authentication and authorization to our app. Let's do that.

Adding API Authentication

We'll start by adding the required code to authorize the API. To organize our code well, we are going to add a new project that contains all our authentication.

Create the Authentication Library

1. Right-click the Solution, select Add, and click New Project.

2. Select Class Library and click "Next."

3. Name the project "StaticWebAppAuthentication" and click "Next."

4. Select ".Net 6.0 (Long-term support)" for the framework and click "Create."

5. Delete the "Class1.cs" file.

6. Next, we need to add a model for the ClientPrincipal.

    Right-click the "StaticWebAppAuthentication" folder, click "Add," and select "New Folder."

7. Name the new folder "Models."

8. Right-click the "Models" folder, click "Add," and select "Class."

9. Call the class "ClientPrincipal."

10. Replace the code in the new class with the code snippet from Code 9-3.

Code 9-3. ClientPrincipal Model

```
namespace StaticWebAppAuthentication.Models;

public class ClientPrincipal
{
    public string IdentityProvider { get; set; }
    public string UserId { get; set; }
    public string UserDetails { get; set; }
    public IEnumerable<string> UserRoles { get; set; }
}
```

As the method that we will make to extract the ClientPrincipal needs access to the request headers, we will add the "Microsoft.AspNetCore.Http" NuGet package.

1. In the "StaticWebAppAuthentication" project, right-click the Dependencies folder and click "Manage NuGet Packages…".

2. Go to the "Browse" tab.

3. Search for "Microsoft.AspNetCore.Http".

4. Click "Install."

5. On the "Preview Change" window, click "OK."

6. On the "License Acceptance" window, click "I Accept."

Now we can create the method we will be using in the Api project.

1. Right-click the "StaticWebAppAuthentication" project, click "Add," and select "Folder."

2. Name the folder "Api."

3. Right-click the new folder, click "Add," and select "Class."

4. Name the new class "StaticWebAppApiAuthorization."

5. Replace the code with the code snippet from Code 9-4.

Code 9-4. StaticWebAppApiAuthorization Class

```
using System.Text;
using System.Text.Json;
using Microsoft.AspNetCore.Http;
using StaticWebAppAuthentication.Models;

namespace StaticWebAppAuthentication.Api;

public static class StaticWebAppApiAuthorization
{
    public static ClientPrincipal ➥
        ParseHttpHeaderForClientPrincipal
            (IHeaderDictionary headers)
```

```
{
    if (!headers.TryGetValue ➡
        ("x-ms-client-principal", out var header))
    {
        return new ClientPrincipal();
    }

    var data = header[0];
    var decoded = Convert.FromBase64String(data);
    var json = Encoding.UTF8.GetString(decoded);
    var principal = ➡
        JsonSerializer.Deserialize<ClientPrincipal>(
        json,
        new JsonSerializerOptions ➡
        { PropertyNameCaseInsensitive = true });

    return principal ?? new ClientPrincipal();
    }
}
```

This function takes in an "IHeaderDictionary," which we will take from the request in our API call.

We try to extract the "x-ms-client-principal" header from the dictionary – this is the header that the Azure Static Web App adds to our request before it arrives at our Api.

If the header doesn't exist, then we return an empty ClientPrincipal, which means that the user is not authenticated.

This header is a StringValues object, but we are only interested in the first entry. This is the Base64 encoded JSON string. After converting to a standard JSON string, we deserialize the JSON to our C# object.

Finally, we check if the ClientPrincipal exists before returning it. If it doesn't exist, we return a new ClientPrincipal. Again, this means that our user will not be authenticated for the request.

Add Authentication Library to the Api Project

Now that our library code is correct, we can add the project reference to our Api library.

1. In the Api project, right-click the Dependencies folder and click "Add Project Dependency"; see Figure 9-2.

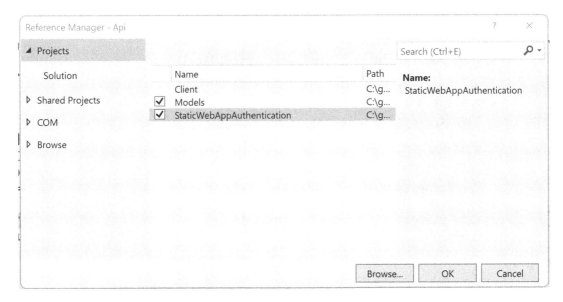

Figure 9-2. *Add Project Dependencies to the Api Project*

2. Ensure that the "StaticWebAppAuthentication" project is selected and click "OK."

The Api project now has authentication and authorization available!

Client-Side Authentication

The client-side application requires works differently to the API. Before we can start coding, we need another NuGet package in our "StaticWebAppAuthentication" project.

1. In the "StaticWebAppAuthentication" project, right-click the "Dependencies" folder and click "Manage NuGet Packages."

2. Go to the Browse tab.

3. Search for "Microsoft.AspNetCore.Components.Authorization".

    Ensure that you install the latest stable 6.x version of the package and not the prerelease version 7.x. Ensure that the "Include prerelease" checkbox is unchecked.

4. Click "Install."

5. On the "Preview Change" window, click "OK."

6. On the "License Acceptance" window, click "I Accept."

To implement client-side authentication, we need a new class in our new "Models" folder.

1. In the "StaticWebAppAuthentication" project, right-click the "Models" folder, click "Add," and select "Class."

2. Name the class "AuthenticationData."

3. Replace the contents of the file with the code snippet from Code 9-5.

Code 9-5. AuthenticationData Class

```
namespace StaticWebAppAuthentication.Models;

public class AuthenticationData
{
    public ClientPrincipal ClientPrincipal { get; set; }
}
```

Next, we need the code to process the ClientPrincipal for the Blazor application.

1. Right-click the "StaticWebAppAuthentication" project, click "Add," and select "New Folder."

2. Name the folder "Client."

3. Right-click the "Client" folder, click "Add," and select "Class."

4. Name the class "StaticWebAppsAuthenticationStateProvider."

5. Replace the code with the code snippet from Code 9-6.

Code 9-6. StaticWebAppsAuthenticationStateProvider

```
using Microsoft.AspNetCore.Components.Authorization;
using StaticWebAppAuthentication.Models;
using System.Net.Http.Json;
using System.Security.Claims;

namespace StaticWebAppAuthentication.Client;

public class StaticWebAppsAuthenticationStateProvider : ➥
    AuthenticationStateProvider
{
    private readonly HttpClient http;

    public StaticWebAppsAuthenticationStateProvider ➥
        (HttpClient httpClient)
    {
        ArgumentNullException.ThrowIfNull ➥
            (httpClient, nameof(httpClient));
        this.http = httpClient; }
}
```

In the constructor of the class, we are injecting the HttpClient that we also used to retrieve the blog posts in an earlier chapter and checking that it's not null.

The class itself is inherited from "AuthenticationStateProvider." This allows us to inject the state into our Client application.

We have a red squiggly line on the screen now; this is because we have not implemented the method required by the "AuthenticationStateProvider." We'll implement that later in this section.

Next, we need to retrieve the ClientPrincipal itself.

6. Add the code snippet from Code 9-7 to the class below the constructor.

Code 9-7. GetClientPrincipal Code Snippet

```
private async Task<ClientPrincipal> GetClientPrincipal()
{
    var data = await http.GetFromJsonAsync ➥
            <AuthenticationData>("/.auth/me");
    var clientPrincipal = data?.ClientPrincipal ?? ➥
            new ClientPrincipal();
    return clientPrincipal;
}
```

We make a call to the "./auth/me" endpoint to retrieve the JSON ClientPrincipal object. As mentioned, we can do this because this call will happen from inside of the browser and so uses the authentication cookie set by the Azure Static Web App.

Next, we try to deserialize this JSON object into a ClientPrincipal object. If the call has returned value data, then we have a ClientPrincipal to return; otherwise, we have a null object.

In the case of the latter, we return a new ClientPrincipal object. This indicates that we do not have an authenticated user.

So that the ClientPrincipal can be used in our Blazor application, we need to convert it to a ClaimsPrincipal.

7. Add the code snippet from Code 9-8 to the class after the constructor.

Code 9-8. GetClaimsFromClientClaimsPrincipal

```
public static ClaimsPrincipal ➥
    GetClaimsFromClientClaimsPrincipal ➥
    (ClientPrincipal principal)
{
    principal.UserRoles =
        principal.UserRoles?.Except ➥
        (new[] { "anonymous" }, ➥
        StringComparer.CurrentCultureIgnoreCase) ➥
        ?? new List<string>();
```

```
    if (!principal.UserRoles.Any())
    {
        return new ClaimsPrincipal();
    }

    ClaimsIdentity identity = ➡
        AdaptToClaimsIdentity(principal);
    return new ClaimsPrincipal(identity);
}
```

Earlier in the chapter, we covered that an authenticated user will always have two roles, "anonymous" and "authenticated." The "anonymous" role doesn't really give us much information about the user. Should the user only have that role, then we want to treat them as unauthenticated because we do not really know who they are.

The first step is to strip out that role. At the same time, we are also checking that we have a UserRoles list at all – and if we don't just create an empty list.

Next, we check how many UserRoles the user has. If it is zero, then we return an empty ClaimsPrincipal. This means that the user will not be treated as authenticated inside of the application.

If we do have UserRoles, then we want to adapt the ClientPrincipal to a ClaimsIdentity and use that ClaimsIdentity to create the ClaimsPrincipal that we will use in the application.

We still need the code to adapt the ClientPrincipal to a ClaimsIdentity.

8. Add the code snippet from Code 9-9 under the "GetClaimsFromClientClaimsPrincipal" function.

Code 9-9. GetClaimsFromClientClaimsPrincipal

```
private static ClaimsIdentity AdaptToClaimsIdentity(ClientPrincipal
principal)
{
    var identity =
        new ClaimsIdentity(principal.IdentityProvider);
    identity.AddClaim(
        new Claim(
            ClaimTypes.NameIdentifier,
            principal.UserId!));
```

```
identity.AddClaim(
    new Claim(
        ClaimTypes.Name,
        principal.UserDetails!));

identity.AddClaims(
    principal.UserRoles!
    .Select(r => new Claim(ClaimTypes.Role, r)));

return identity;
}
```

We create a ClaimsIdentity based on the IdentityProvider field of the ClientPrincipal. Then we add two special claims: the NameIdentifier based on the userId, which is the user id created for us by the Azure Static Web App, and the Name based on the UserDetails, which is the information returned from the external authentication provider.

Finally, we add the roles in the ClientPrincipal before returning the ClaimsIdentity.

The only thing that we need to do now is to use this in a way that sets the AuthenticationState in the application.

9. Add the code snippet from Code 9-10 below the constructor in the class.

Code 9-10. GetAuthenticationStateAsync

```
public override async Task<AuthenticationState> ➥
        GetAuthenticationStateAsync()
{
    try
    {
        var clientPrincipal = ➥
            await GetClientPrincipal();
        var claimsPrincipal = ➥
                GetClaimsFromClientClaimsPrincipal ➥
                (clientPrincipal);
        return new ➥
            AuthenticationState(claimsPrincipal);
    }
```

```
    catch
    {
        return new AuthenticationState ➥
                    (new ClaimsPrincipal());
    }
}
```

By using the methods that we already wrote, we can make this function short.

First, we get the ClientPrincipal and convert it to the ClaimsPrincipal. Then we return a new AuthenticationState using that ClaimsPrincipal.

If there are any errors, we revert to classing the user as not authenticated in the "Catch" block.

Now we have an authentication step that we can use in our application.

1. In the "StaticWebAppAuthentication" project, right-click the "Client" folder, click "Add," and select "Class."

2. Name the class "StaticWebAppAuthenticationExtensions."

3. Replace the code in the class with the code snippet from Code 9-11.

Code 9-11. StaticWebAppAuthenticationExtensions Class

```
using Microsoft.AspNetCore.Components.Authorization;
using Microsoft.Extensions.DependencyInjection;

namespace StaticWebAppAuthentication.Client;

public static class StaticWebAppAuthenticationExtensions
{
    public static IServiceCollection ➥
        AddStaticWebAppsAuthentication ➥
        (this IServiceCollection services)    `
    {
        return services
```

```
        .AddAuthorizationCore()
        .AddScoped<AuthenticationStateProvider, ➥
        StaticWebAppsAuthenticationStateProvider>();
    }
}
```

This class adds two things to the Services available in our application. "AddAuthorizationCore" adds, as the name suggests, core authorization to our application so that we can use it inside of our code.

The "AddScoped" function injects our new "StaticWebAppsAuthenticationStateProvider" to be used when the application needs an "AuthenticationStateProvider." This allows us to use our ClaimsPrincipal in our application.

This was a lot of code for us to create, but we are finally ready to use it in our application!

Add Authentication Library to Client Project

Before we get started with authentication in our pages, we are going to add authentication to the client application itself.

We need to add "Microsoft.AspNetCore.Components.Authorization" to our Client application. This allows Blazor to work with authentication and authorization.

1. In the "Client" project, right-click "Dependencies," and select "Manage NuGet Packages."

2. Click the "Browse" tab.

3. Search for and select the latest stable version 6.x of "Microsoft.AspNetCore.Components.Authorization".

4. Click "Install."

5. On the "Preview Changes" window, click "OK."

6. On the "License Acceptance" window, click "I Accept."

Next, we need to reference our "StaticWebAppAuthentication" project, as we did for the Api project.

1. In the "Client" project, right-click the "Dependencies" folder, and select "Add Project Reference."

2. Ensure that the "StaticWebAppAuthentication" folder is checked and click "OK."

3. In the "Client" project, open "Program.cs".

4. Add the code snippet from Code 9-12 to the top of the file under the existing "using" statements.

Code 9-12. Using Statement for StaticWebAppAuthentication.Client;

```
using StaticWebAppAuthentication.Client;
```

5. Under the line where we added the "BlogPostSummaryService" and "BlogPostService," add the code snippet from Code 9-13.

Code 9-13. Adding the AuthenticationStateManager to builder.Services

```
builder.Services.AddStaticWebAppsAuthentication();
```

The last thing we need to do before we start adding code is to add authentication to the router for our application.

But we also need to update our "_imports.razor" file for this.

1. Open the "_imports.razor".

2. Add the code snippet from Code 9-14 to the end of the file.

Code 9-14. Import for Microsoft.AspNetCore.Components.Authorization

```
@using Microsoft.AspNetCore.Components.Authorization
```

3. In the "Client" project root folder, open "App.razor".

4. At the top of the page, add the tag from Code 9-15.

Code 9-15. CascadingAuthenticationState Tag

```
<CascadingAuthenticationState>
```

5. Add the corresponding closing tag, Code 9-16, to the bottom of the file.

Code 9-16. Closing CascadingAuthenticationState Tag

```
</CascadingAuthenticationState>
```

These tags ensure that we have our authentication state available in every razor component in our application. Let's put it to use!

Login Screen

Now we need to add the interactive element so that our users can log in and log out with more ease and to show their status without manually going to the "./auth/me" resource.

1. In the "Client" project, right-click the "Pages" folder, click "Add," and select "Razor Component."

2. Name the component "Login.razor".

3. Replace the contents of the file with the code snippet from Code 9-17.

Code 9-17. Login.razor Component

```
@page "/login"

<PageTitle>Login</PageTitle>

@{
    var providers = new Dictionary<string, string>
    {
        { "aad", "Microsoft" },
        { "github", "GitHub" },
        { "twitter", "Twitter" },
        { "google", "Google"}
    };
}

<h1>Login</h1>
```

```
<div>
    @foreach(var provider in providers)
    {
        <div>
            <a class="btn btn-block btn-lg btn-social ➡
                btn-@provider.Key" ➡
                href="/.auth/login/@provider.Key">
                <span class="fab fa-@provider.Key"> ➡
                </span>
                Sign in with @provider.Value
            </a>
        </div>
    }
</div>
```

This page will put four different login buttons on the screen. One for each of the providers that we have. The buttons link to the built-in login resources that Azure Static Web Apps provide us out of the box.

We are using this extra page just to give easy access to each of the providers; if only one provider is needed, then we can just link directly to it from the navigation menu and skip that extra page.

We'll provide a link to this page in the navigation menu of our website.

1. In the "Client" project, in the "Shared" folder, open the "NavMenu. razor" file.

2. Under the navigation for the blog post overview page, add the code snippet from Code 9-18.

Code 9-18. Login Navigation

```
<AuthorizeView>
    <Authorized>
        <div class="nav-item px-3">
            <NavLink class="nav-link" ➡
                href="/.auth/logout?➡
                post_logout_redirect_uri=/">
                <span class="oi oi-account-logout" ➡
```

```
                    aria-hidden="true"></span>
                @(context.User.HasClaim(➡
                    c => c.Value == "admin") ? ➡
                    "(Admin) Logout" : ➡
                    "Logout")
            </NavLink>
        </div>
    </Authorized>
    <NotAuthorized>
        <div class="nav-item px-3">
            <NavLink class="nav-link" ➡
                href="/login ">
                <span class="oi oi-account-login" ➡
                    aria-hidden="true"></span> Login
            </NavLink>
        </div>
    </NotAuthorized>
</AuthorizeView>
```

This is the first use of authentication in our site!

The "AuthorizeView" tag is what gives us access to our authentication information. Inside we have two routes: "Authorized" for when we are authenticated and "NotAuthorized" for when not.

When we first visit the site and haven't logged in, we see the "NotAuthorized" route. And so, we have our link to the login page that we just created.

However, when we are logged in, we change the navigation link to allow us to log out.

We've also given a bit of feedback regarding the status of the user in the logout button. If the user has the special role "admin," then we display "(Admin)" in the logout button.

That is all the code that we need to make authentication and authorization information available for our application – along with a simple way to access that login information for users.

Let's deploy our updated application.

In the "Git Changes" window, commit the altered files with a comment and push to GitHub.

The last thing that we are going to look at in this chapter is how to add that special "admin" role that we are using in the application. This is also how we are going to ensure that now all authenticated users can create/edit blog posts in the next chapter.

Role-Based Access

At the start of the chapter, we looked at the roles that each user has when authenticating in an Azure Static Web App: "anonymous" and "authenticated." These are important to allow us to recognize if the user is known or not.

But when we need extra control, we can add extra roles, like the "admin" role used for the login button.

When using the free tier, as we are doing, these roles are controlled in the Azure Portal.

1. Open the Portal and go to the Azure Static Web App created for this book.

2. On the left-hand side of the screen, under "Settings" there is a link for "Role management"; see Figure 9-3.
   Click the link to open the Role management screen.

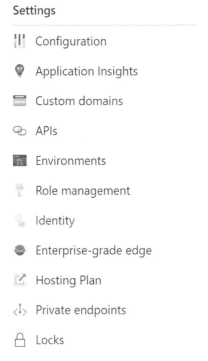

Figure 9-3. *Azure Portal Settings for Azure Static Web Apps*

In the Role management screen, Figure 9-4, we can invite new users to the site, manage users that are already invited, or remove users.

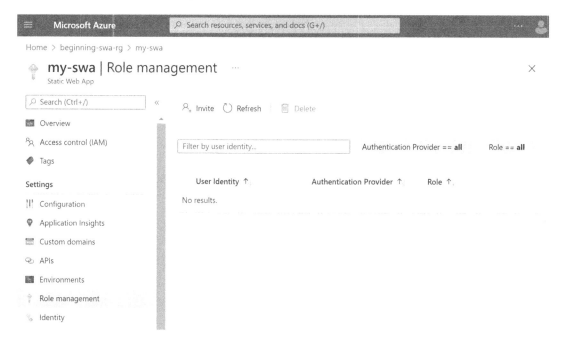

Figure 9-4. *Role Management for Azure Static Web Apps*

Using this screen, we can, at the time of writing, assign special roles to up to 25 users using the Azure Portal. This doesn't seem much, but we need to remember that we only need to add users with something other than the standard "anonymous" and "authenticated" roles. None of our other users need to be added to the portal. For many applications, 25 users with special roles will be enough.

For those applications where it is not, a standard tier app can be used with an Azure Function to handle roles. But that is outside of the scope for this book.

3. To add a user, click the invite link, seen in Figure 9-4, to open the "Create invitation link" fly-in.

    This can be seen in Figure 9-5.

Create invitation link   ✕

Invitation links grant specific users access to your domain. You can specify when the links expire.

Authentication provider * | Azure Active Directory   ∨ |

Email address * | |

Domain * | agreeable-wave-01cef0403.1.azurestaticap...   ∨ |

Role * | contributor,reader |

Invitation expiration (in hours) * ⓘ | 1 |

| Generate | | Close |

Figure 9-5. *Azure Static Web App Invite Fly-In*

We need five bits of information here:

- The authentication provider that is going to be used

- The user handle/email for the authentication provider

- The domain for the user

- The role(s) for the user as a comma-separated list

- How long the invite should stay valid

4. Fill in the details of the user to invite.
   In the example of Figure 9-6, my GitHub details have been used.
   Remember that the role needs to be "admin," with lowercase letters.

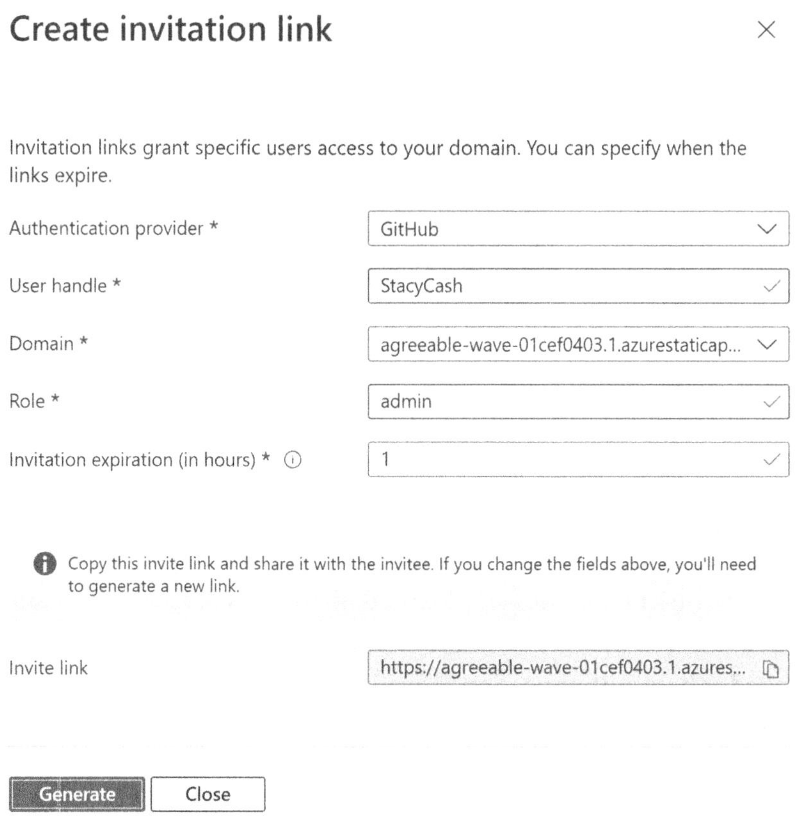
Create invitation link
Invitation links grant specific users access to your domain. You can specify when the links expire.
Authentication provider *
GitHub
User handle *
StacyCash
Domain *
agreeable-wave-01cef0403.1.azurestaticap...
Role *
admin
Invitation expiration (in hours) *
1
Copy this invite link and share it with the invitee. If you change the fields above, you'll need to generate a new link.
Invite link
https://agreeable-wave-01cef0403.1.azures...
Generate
Close

Figure 9-6. *Completed Create Invite Link Fly-In*

5. Click "Generate"; the screen should look a little like Figure 9-6.

6. Copy the invite link using the copy icon in the link text box and paste it into a new tab in the browser.

If the user is not already logged in to the account specified in the fly-out, then log in and grant consent to the Azure Static Web App if requested, and the website should load.

If our changes have been deployed, then we should now see a logout button with the "(Admin)" text inside of it as in Figure 9-7.

Figure 9-7. *Logout Button with Admin Text*

We are now ready to use our authentication to complete the project!

Conclusion

Over the course of this chapter, we have learned about using the standard authentication that we get out of the box with Azure Static Web Apps.

We've looked at how authentication is available without having to write any code, what information they give to us about the user, and what providers we have available to us.

We've looked at role management in the Azure Portal, allowing us to use role-based access control inside of our application.

Finally, we have added a library that allows us to use this functionality inside of our application – both on the Client, where we now have login functionality available, and in the API.

Now that we can secure our application, we are ready to add the functionality that will create and edit blog posts in the next chapter.

The source code for this book is available on GitHub, located at `https://github.com/Apress/beginning-azure-static-web-apps`. For the completed code for this chapter, see the "chapter-9" folder.

CHAPTER 10

Creating Blog Posts

In the previous chapter, we implemented authentication and authorization in our application and registered a user with admin rights. Now we can get our application completed!

Our application takes blog posts from our CosmosDB and displays them to the user. Right now though, we need to create and edit blog posts inside of the CosmosDB – by manipulating the JSON data directly. That isn't the most user-friendly way of working – and there is a good chance that we can break something.

In this chapter, we are going to create functionality that allows a user with the "admin" role to create and edit blog posts inside of the application. We'll do this by adding an editable form to the application, sending new and edited blog posts via our Azure Functions to the CosmosDB and ensuring that only users with the "admin" role have access to the functionality.

Technical Requirements

To complete the steps in this chapter, you will need to have the Azure Account created in Chapter 2, a deployed Azure Static Web App from Chapter 4, and the application from Chapter 9 available in a GitHub repository.

The source code for this book is available on GitHub, located at `https://github.com/Apress/beginning-azure-static-web-apps`. For this chapter, use the "chapter-9" folder for the start code.

Adding the Azure Functions

Before we can make the changes to the Client application for the user interaction, we are going to make three new functions in our Api project.

© Stacy Cashmore 2022
S. Cashmore, *Beginning Azure Static Web Apps*, https://doi.org/10.1007/978-1-4842-8146-8_10

We are building a REST (Representational State Transfer) interface for our Azure Functions; the same endpoint we already built to retrieve blog posts is going to manage our data differently depending on how it is being called.

The methods that we have available are

- GET: Fetch data from the server.

  We are using this to display the blog posts.

- POST: Create data on the server.

  We will use this for creating new blog posts.

- PUT: Replace data on the server.

  We will use this for updating blog posts.

- DELETE: Remove data from the server.

  We will use this for deleting blog posts.

- PATCH: Modify the contents of data on the server.

  We won't be using this method in the book, but could be used to update only part of the blog posts.

Creating Blog Posts with the POST Method

The first endpoint that we will create will use the POST method, used for creating data on the server. This function will accept a blog post without an ID, create that ID, add the user who is creating the post as the author, create the document in our CosmosDB container, and return the ID.

To do this, we are going to take advantage of the CosmosDB bindings available to us in Azure Functions.

Azure Functions have a multitude of bindings available out of the box to make our lives easier – but not all can be used with Azure Static Web Apps. When using new bindings, always make sure to research it first to check for compatibility.

1. In the "Api" project, open the "BlogPosts.cs" file.

2. Add the code snippet from Code 10-1 under the "using" statements at the top of the file.

Code 10-1. PostBlogPost "using" Statements

```
using System;
using Microsoft.Azure.Cosmos;
using System.Threading.Tasks;
using StaticWebAppAuthentication.Api;
using StaticWebAppAuthentication.Models;
```

3. Under the GetBlogPost function, add the code snippet from Code 10-2.

Code 10-2. Azure Function Method Declaration for Creating a Blog Post

```
[FunctionName($"{nameof(BlogPosts)}_Post")]
public static IActionResult PostBlogPost(
    [HttpTrigger(AuthorizationLevel.Anonymous, "post",
        Route = "blogposts")]
    BlogPost blogPost,
    HttpRequest request,
    [CosmosDB("SwaBlog",
        "BlogContainer",
        Connection = "CosmosDbConnectionString")]
    out dynamic savedBlogPost,
    ILogger log)
{}
```

This declares the Azure Function, using an HTTP POST on the "blogposts" endpoint. We pass three parameters into the Azure Function:

- A Blogpost object deserialized from the request body

- The HttpRequest, the data associated with the request itself

- An out parameter for the CosmosDB document that we will save

Whatever object we put into the document will be saved to the CosmosDB when the Azure Function exits.

4. Add the code snippet from Code 10-3 into the function created using Code 10-2.

Code 10-3. PostBlogPost Method Body

```
if (blogPost.Id != default)
{
    savedBlogPost = null;
    return new BadRequestObjectResult("id must be null");
}

var clientPrincipal =
    StaticWebAppApiAuthorization
    .ParseHttpHeaderForClientPrincipal(request.Headers);

blogPost.Id = Guid.NewGuid();
blogPost.Author = clientPrincipal.UserDetails;

savedBlogPost = new
{
    id = blogPost.Id.ToString(),
    Title = blogPost.Title,
    Author = blogPost.Author,
    PublishedDate = blogPost.PublishedDate,
    Tags = blogPost.Tags,
    BlogPostMarkdown = blogPost.BlogPostMarkdown,
    Status = 2
};
return new OkObjectResult(blogPost);
```

We check that there isn't an Id already set for the blog post because we are using the POST function to create our blog post.

If a blog post already has an Id, then we set the CosmosDB document to null and return a 400 response indicating that there is a problem with the request. Setting the document to null will stop it from being saved to the CosmosDB.

Next, we extract the ClientPrincipal from the request header and use it to fill the Author field.

We are setting the Author directly from the authorization details here. This is not something that we should do in the real world. Rather, there should be functionality to link the UserId to a display name, but that is outside of the scope of this book.

Be aware that if a post is created for a user authenticated with either Google or Azure Active Directory, the email will be exposed when displaying the blog post.

And the final preparation step is to create a new Id for the blog post.

Then we set the document, including the author and Id, so that it can be saved to the CosmosDB when the function completes.

The updated BlogPost object is then returned from the function so that it can be used, with the extra information for the Id and Author, by the calling party.

Updating Blog Posts with the PUT HTTP Method

Sometimes, we'll make mistakes in our blog posts and need to edit them. To support that, we will add a new function, using the PUT HTTP method. This method allows us to replace data on the server.

1. Add the code from Code 10-4 and paste it under the POST function we just created.

Code 10-4. Azure Function Method Declaration for Replacing a Blog Post

```
[FunctionName($"{nameof(BlogPosts)}_Put")]
public static IActionResult PutBlogPost(
    [HttpTrigger(AuthorizationLevel.Anonymous, "put",
        Route = "blogposts")]
    BlogPost updatedBlogPost,
    [CosmosDB("SwaBlog",
        "BlogContainer",
        Connection = "CosmosDbConnectionString",
        Id = "{Id}",
        PartitionKey = "{Author}")]
    BlogPost currentBlogPost,
    [CosmosDB("SwaBlog",
        "BlogContainer",
        Connection = "CosmosDbConnectionString")]
```

```
    out dynamic savedBlogPost,
    ILogger log)
{}
```

This Azure Function declaration sets the HTTP trigger for the PUT method. As with the POST method, we pass in three parameters:

- The BlogPost object we are trying to update

- The current version of the BlogPost that we are trying to update

- An out parameter for the CosmosDB document that we will save

As we do not need the ClientPrincipal for this function, we do not need the full HttpRequest object.

We also try to load the current BlogPost from the CosmosDB, based on the Id and Author of the inbound document.

We have the same output dynamic document as we had in our previous function. Now we can build the body of the function to do the work.

2. Copy the code from Code 10-5 into the function body at the end of Code 10-4.

Code 10-5. PutBlogPost Method Body

```
if (currentBlogPost is null)
{
    savedBlogPost = null;
    return new NotFoundResult();
}

savedBlogPost = new
{
    id = updatedBlogPost.Id.ToString(),
    Title = updatedBlogPost.Title,
    Author = updatedBlogPost.Author,
    PublishedDate = updatedBlogPost.PublishedDate,
    Tags = updatedBlogPost.Tags,
```

```
        BlogPostMarkdown = updatedBlogPost.BlogPostMarkdown,
        Status = 2
};
return new NoContentResult();
```

The PUT function is used to replace data in our database, so we will replace the entire CosmosDB document when we make a change, for example, when we edit a blog post.

To ensure that we are not saving data incorrectly, we check that the currentBlogPost parameter isn't null. If it is, then we return a "Not Found" result, setting the output document variable to null so that nothing is saved to the CosmosDB.

If the currentBlogPost parameter is set, then we can replace the data. We set the output document in the same way as we do when creating a blog post. As the ID and the author are the same, the original blog post will be overwritten with the new data.

As there is no new information to return to the calling party when changing data, we return a no content result. This indicates that we have successfully completed the request, but that there is no data to return.

Deleting Blog Posts with the DELETE HTTP Method

The last use case that we are going to handle is removing blog posts. To handle this, we are going to use the DELETE HTTP method.

1. Copy the code snippet from Code 10-6 and paste it under the function we created with Code 10-5.

Code 10-6. Azure Function Method Declaration for Deleting a Blog Post

```
[FunctionName($"{nameof(BlogPosts)}_Delete")]
public static async Task<IActionResult> DeleteBlogPost(
    [HttpTrigger(AuthorizationLevel.Anonymous, "delete",
        Route = "blogposts/{author}/{id}")]
    HttpRequest request,
    string author,
    string id,
```

```
    [CosmosDB(
        "SwaBlog",
        "BlogContainer",
        Connection = "CosmosDbConnectionString",
        Id = "{id}",
        PartitionKey = "{author}")]
    BlogPost currentBlogPost,
    [CosmosDB(Connection = "CosmosDbConnectionString")]
    CosmosClient client,
    ILogger log)
{}
```

The HTTP trigger is linked to the DELETE HTTP method, but we pass in more parameters for this function:

- The HttpRequest, as it's a requirement of the HTTP trigger

- The id parameter from the URL

- The author parameter from the URL

- The current version of the BlogPost that we are trying to delete

- A CosmosClient object for accessing our CosmosDB container

Those URL parameters are also used to match the route of the request, as we do when fetching a full blog post using the ID.

Using these parameters, we can safely delete the BlogPost.

We have a different return type for this function, rather than the IActionResult that we have used in the other functions; this time, we are returning a Task<IActionResult>. This is because for the delete we need to use asynchronous development.

2. Copy the snippet from Code 10-7 into the function created with Code 10-6.

Code 10-7. DeleteBlogPost Method Body

```
if (currentBlogPost is null)
{
    return new NoContentResult();
}
```

```
Container container =
    client.GetDatabase("SwaBlog")
    .GetContainer("BlogContainer");
await container
    .DeleteItemAsync<BlogPost>(id, new PartitionKey(author));

return new NoContentResult();
```

We again check to see if we have found the blog post that we are trying to delete. We do it for a different reason when deleting though. The function of the delete is to ensure that the data isn't in our CosmosDB. If we don't find the data, then we can simply return the NoContentResult to indicate success – after all, the document doesn't exist, which is our target state.

We need this extra step to ensure that the CosmosDB doesn't return an error when trying to remove nonexistent data.

If the data is found, we can send the request to delete it using the CosmosClient parameter we passed into the function. If this returns without error, we can return the NoContentResult.

Securing the Functions

In our three new functions, we are only using the authentication data to set the author when creating and updating a blog post. We have not used it yet to determine if the user has the rights to access the functions themselves.

Rather than secure the functions directly, we are going to use that glue inside of the Azure Static Web App again. We looked at the way the "staticwebapp.config.json" can help us set up the routes in our application, including setting up access control.

As the API is never called directly, but always through the Azure Static Web App, this works for both access to static resources on the server and API endpoints.

Because of this, we need to make changes to the "staticwebapp.settings.json" file in the Client project to secure the API itself.

We can check this by using the "routes" object in the "staticwebapp.config.json" file.

1. In the Client project, in the "wwwroot" folder, open the "staticwebapp.config.json" file.

2. Add the code from Code 10-8 above the navigation fallback object.

Code 10-8. Route Configuration in the staticwebapp.config.json File

```
"routes": [
    {
        "route": "/api/blogposts",
        "methods": ["POST", "PUT", "DELETE"],
        "allowedRoles": ["admin"]
    }
],
```

This configuration ensures that any user can access the HTTP GET functions, either to retrieve the blog post summaries or a full individual blog post, but cannot call the POST, PUT, or DELETE methods to change the data unless they have the "admin" role.

Having this rule in place will ensure that the API is kept secure, without having to handle the authentication ourselves in our code. This makes our code simpler, more secure, and easier to maintain.

These are all the changes needed to secure the Api project. Next, we'll add the create and edit functionality to the Client application.

Updating the Blog Post Services

We are going to add functionality to the two blog post services we created back in Chapter 7. These changes have two functions. They will interact with the new Azure Functions that we have just created. They will also ensure that the data inside of our Client application running in the browser remains up to date with the changes that we are making without making extraneous HTTP requests.

Creating Blog Posts

First, we'll add the code to create new blog posts.

BlogPostService Changes

Inside of the BlogPostService, we need to add the code to communicate with the Azure Function to create the BlogPost.

Before we add the function though, we need to make some changes to the class to prepare for it.

1. In the Client project, under the "Services" folder, open the "BlogPostService.cs" file.

2. Add the using statement from Code 10-9 to the top of the file.

Code 10-9. Extra Using Statement for BlogPostService.cs

```
using System.Text;
using System.Text.Json;
```

3. Add a private variable to hold the reference to the BlogPostSummaryService.

Copy the code snippet from Code 10-10 under the last private variable in the BlogPostService class.

Code 10-10. Private Variable for BlogPostSummaryService

```
private readonly BlogPostSummaryService ➡
    blogPostSummaryService;
```

4. Change the constructor of the BlogPostService to match the code snippet in Code 10-11.

This will inject the BlogPostSummaryService into our class.

Code 10-11. Updated Constructor for BlogPostService

```
public BlogPostService(
    HttpClient http,
    NavigationManager navigationManager,
    BlogPostSummaryService blogPostSummaryService)
{
    ArgumentNullException.ThrowIfNull(http, nameof(http));
    ArgumentNullException.ThrowIfNull(
        navigationManager,
        nameof(navigationManager));
    ArgumentNullException.ThrowIfNull(
        blogPostSummaryService,
        nameof(blogPostSummaryService));
```

```
    this.http = http;
    this.navigationManager = navigationManager;
    this.blogPostSummaryService = blogPostSummaryService;
}
```

Now the BlogPostService has been prepared, we can add the functions themselves.

5. Add the CreateBlogPost function from Code 10-12 to the end of
    the class.

Code 10-12. CreateBlogPost Function

```
public async Task<BlogPost> Create(BlogPost blogPost)
{
    ArgumentNullException
        .ThrowIfNull(blogPost, nameof(blogPost));

    var content = JsonSerializer.Serialize(blogPost);
    var data = new StringContent➡
        (content, Encoding.UTF8, "application/json");

    var result = await http.PostAsync➡
        ("api/blogposts", data);
    result.EnsureSuccessStatusCode();

    BlogPost? savedBlogPost = await ➡
        result.Content.ReadFromJsonAsync<BlogPost>();
    blogPostCache.Add(savedBlogPost!);
    blogPostSummaryService.Add(savedBlogPost!);

    return savedBlogPost!;
}
```

First, we check that valid data has been passed into the service; if not, we throw an error.

Then we convert the BlogPost to StringContent that we can use as the body of the POST request that we send to the Azure Function.

We deserialize the data that we get back and add it to the Client application collection of full blog posts and summaries.

Finally, we return the ID of the blog post we just created.

At the moment, we get a red squiggly as we haven't yet made the changes to the BlogPostSummaryService. We'll do that in the next section.

We will write the code for the summary service next.

BlogPostSummaryService Changes

So that we can find the blog post on our list of summaries, we also need to add the blog post to our BlogPostSummaryService. We already have the call in the BlogPostService class; we just need to create the method now.

1. In the Client project, under the "Services" folder open the "BlogPostSummaryService.cs" file.

2. Add the code from Code 10-13 to the end of the class.

Code 10-13. Add Method for BlogpostSummaryService

```
public void Add(BlogPost blogPost)
{
    ArgumentNullException
        .ThrowIfNull(blogPost, nameof(blogPost));

    if (Summaries is null)
    {
        return;
    }
}
```

The first thing that we need to do in the service is to check that there is anything that we need to do.

We check that a blog post has been passed to the service; if not, we throw an error.

Then we check that the summaries object has been filled – if the user has called the create page directly, then we will not have filled the list from the API yet.

If not, then we simply exit – the first time that the user sees the list of blog posts, it will be loaded from the API, including the blog post we have just written.

3. Add the code snippet from Code 10-14 to the end of the function
   we created with the code snippet from Code 10-13.

Code 10-14. Adding the BlogPost to the Summaries List

```
if (!Summaries.Any(summary =>
    summary.Id == blogPost.Id
    && summary.Author == blogPost.Author))
{
    var summary = new BlogPost
    {
        Id = blogPost.Id,
        Author = blogPost.Author,
        BlogPostMarkdown = blogPost.BlogPostMarkdown,
        PublishedDate = blogPost.PublishedDate,
        Tags = blogPost.Tags,
        Title = blogPost.Title
    };

    if (summary.BlogPostMarkdown?.Length > 500)
    {
        summary.BlogPostMarkdown =
            summary.BlogPostMarkdown[..500];
    }

    Summaries.Add(summary);
}
```

First, we check to see if the blog post already exists in the summaries list.

If not, then we create a new BlogPost using the data we pass in.

We check the length of the blog post itself, and if it's longer than the 500 characters that we have for our summaries, then trim it to the first 500.

We can do this safely because we are using Markdown as the format for our blog posts when storing them. If we add any HTML to our blog post in the future, then this code will need to change as cutting off at 500 characters could mean that the HTML is corrupted.

Finally, we add the blog post to the Summaries list itself.

Updating Blog Posts

To update a blog post, we need slightly different functionality as we are no longer adding the blog post to the services but changing the ones that already exist.

Not only does that change the way that we call the API, using the PUT method rather than the POST method, but the way we process data afterward is different as well.

BlogPostService Changes

1. Open the "BlogPostService.cs" file.

2. Add the code snippet from Code 10-15 to the end of the class.

Code 10-15. Update Method in the BlogPostService

```
public async Task Update(BlogPost blogPost)
{
    ArgumentNullException.ThrowIfNull➡
        (blogPost, nameof(blogPost));

    var content = JsonSerializer.Serialize(blogPost);
    var data = new StringContent➡
        (content, Encoding.UTF8, "application/json");

    var result =
        await http.PutAsync("api/blogposts", data);
    result.EnsureSuccessStatusCode();

    int index = blogPostCache.FindIndex(
        bp => bp.Id == blogPost.Id
        && bp.Author == blogPost.Author);
    if (index >= 0)
    {
        blogPostCache[index] = blogPost;
    }

    blogPostSummaryService.Replace(blogPost);
}
```

We start, as with the add functionality, by checking that we have a blog post passed into the method, and if not, then we throw an error.

Then we prepare the PUT statement by converting the BlogPost object to a StringContent object for the body of the PUT request.

Once the blog post has been saved, we search for the index of the original version in the list of BlogPosts in the service. If found, we replace the blog post with the updated version passed into the function.

Finally, we ensure that the list of summaries has also been updated with the new content.

Again, we get a red squiggly line here as we haven't yet made the change to the BlogPostSummaryService. We'll do that in the next section.

BlogPostSummaryService Changes

1. Open the "BlogPostSummaryService.cs" file.

2. Add the code snippet from Code 10-16 to the end of the class.

Code 10-16. Replace Function for BlogPostSummaryService

```
public void Replace(BlogPost blogPost)
{
    ArgumentNullException
            .ThrowIfNull(blogPost, nameof(blogPost));

    if (Summaries == null || !Summaries.Any(➡
        bp => bp.Id == blogPost.Id ➡
        && bp.Author == blogPost.Author))
    {
        return;
    }
}
```

As with our other functions, we first make sure that we have a blog post passed into the function; otherwise, we throw an error.

Then we check to see if the Summaries have been filled yet. As with the Add function, if these have not yet been loaded, then we don't need to do anything – when the visitor goes to the blog post list, it will be filled with all blog posts, including our edited blog post.

3. Add the code snippet from Code 10-17 at the end of the Replace function from Code 10-16.

Code 10-17. Code for the Replace Method in the BlogPostSummaryService

```
var summary = Summaries.Find ➡
    (summary => summary.Id == blogPost.Id
        && summary.Author == blogPost.Author);
if (summary is not null)
{
    summary.Title = blogPost.Title;
    summary.Tags = blogPost.Tags;
    summary.BlogPostMarkdown =
    blogPost.BlogPostMarkdown!;
    if (summary.BlogPostMarkdown.Length > 500)
    {
        summary.BlogPostMarkdown =
            summary.BlogPostMarkdown[..500];
    }
}
```

First, we try to find the existing summary for the blog post.

If we find it, then we change Title, Tags, and Markdown to be the same as the blog post passed into the function.

Finally, we check the length of the Markdown, as we did when adding it originally. If longer than 500 characters, we trim it to the first 500.

Deleting Blog Posts

The last functionality that we need to add to our services is the functionality to delete blog posts.

BlogPostService Changes

1. Open the "BlogPostService.cs" file.

2. Add the code snippet from Code 10-18 to the end of the class.

Code 10-18. Delete Function of the BlogPostService

```
public async Task Delete(Guid id, string author)
{
    var result = await ➥
        http.DeleteAsync($"/api/blogposts/{author}/{id}");
    result.EnsureSuccessStatusCode();

    var blogPost = blogPostCache.FirstOrDefault(➥
        summary => summary.Id == id ➥
        && summary.Author == author);

    if (blogPost is not null)
    {
        blogPostCache.Remove(blogPost);
    }
    blogPostSummaryService.Remove(id, author);
}
```

We call the Delete HTTP Method of the API using the id and author passed into the function.

We then check to see if the post is in the list of BlogPosts held in the service. If it is, we remove it.

Finally, we can remove the associated summary from the BlogPostSummaryService.

As with the previous two functions, we have a red squiggly line. We'll solve this in the next section.

BlogPostSummaryService Changes

1. Open the "BlogPostSummaryService" file.

2. Add the code snippet from Code 10-19 to the end of the class.

Code 10-19. Remove Function of the BlogPostSummaryService

```
public void Remove(Guid id, string author)
{
    if (Summaries == null
        || !Summaries.Any(➥
            summary => summary.Id == id ➥
            && summary.Author == author))
    {
        return;
    }

    var summary =
        Summaries.First(➥
            summary => summary.Id == id ➥
            && summary.Author == author);
    Summaries.Remove(summary);
}
```

We check to see if we have any summaries at all, or if the blog post that we are trying to remove is in the list. If not, we just return – there is no work for us to do.

We then retrieve the summary from the list and remove it.

Now that our services are complete, we can move on to the user interface so that we can finally use our functionality!

Adding the Blog Post Edit Page

We are going to add a page for editing the blog post. This will handle both creation and editing of blog posts in one resource.

1. In the "Client" project, right-click the "Pages" folder. Click "Add" and select "Razor Component…".

2. Call the new component "EditBlogPost.razor".

3. Replace the contents of the file with the code snippet from Code 10-20.

Code 10-20. Attributes for the EditBlogPost.Razor Page

```
@page "/blogposts/{author}/{id}/edit"
@page "/blogposts/{id}/edit"
@using Microsoft.AspNetCore.Authorization
@using Models
@inject BlogPostService service
@inject NavigationManager navigationManager
```

The @page directive sets the URL needed to access our page. Unlike the FullBlogPost page, we are not setting the id parameter to be a GUID. This is because when creating a page, we may not have a GUID to use.

We also have two routes set up. One with the author, and one without. When we are editing a blog post, we have all the information needed to load the blog post, the same as when we are displaying one.

When creating a blog post though, we won't have the author information, and so we need the extra route to take that into account.

We don't force the Id to be a GUID here as when creating a blog post, it will be a string.

Then we add our using statements so that we have access to authentication and model classes.

Finally, we inject the two services that we will be using in the code of the page. The BlogPostService, used for loading, creating, and updating blog posts, and the NavigationManager used to redirect users to the appropriate page after editing has been completed.

We are going to start by adding the code needed to make our page functional.

4. Copy the code snippet from Code 10-21 to the end of the page.

Code 10-21. Properties and Parameters for the EditBlogPost Page

```
@code
{
    private BlogPost? blogPost;
    private string mode = "edit";
    private string tags = string.Empty;
```

```
[Parameter]
public string? Id { get; set; }

[Parameter]
public string? Author {get; set; }
}
```

We have three private variables for the page:

- blogPost: The blog post being edited

- mode: Edit or create. Defaulted to edit

- tags: A variable to hold our processed list of tags for the blog post

We also specify the parameters, Author and Id, passed into the page from the URL. As discussed already, this needs to be a string for when we are creating a new blog post.

5. Add the code snippet from Code 10-22 into the @code block, underneath the Author parameter.

Code 10-22. OnParametersSetAsync for the EditBlogPost Page

```
protected override async Task OnParametersSetAsync()
{
    if (Id == "new")
    {
        mode = "create";
        blogPost = new ();
        return;
    }

    ArgumentNullException.ThrowIfNull
        (Author, nameof(Author));

    if (!Guid.TryParse(Id, out Guid id))
    {
        throw new InvalidCastException();
    }
```

```
    blogPost = await service.GetBlogPost(id, Author);
    tags = String.Join(", ", blogPost!.Tags!);
}
```

If the Id is set to "new," then we set the mode of the page to create. This means that we do not need to load a blog post; we can just set the blogPost object to be a new Blogpost.

If the Id is not "new," then we need to check that we have an Author and valid GUID passed into the page. If not, we throw an error.

If we do have an Author and GUID, then fetch it from the BlogPostService and join the list of Tags from the blog post into one comma-separated string.

After the user has created the blog post, we need to save it.

To ensure that we have a clean set of tags to save, we are going to do some cleanup work before saving them. This will remove any empty tags that the user may have accidentally entered.

6. Copy the code from Code 10-23 to the end of the code block.

Code 10-23. CleanTags Function

```
private string[] CleanTags(string[] tags)
{
    return tags.ToList()
        .Select(tag => tag.Trim())
        .Where(tag => !string.IsNullOrWhiteSpace(tag))
        .ToArray();
}
```

7. Copy the code snippet from Code 10-24 underneath the code snippet from Code 10-23.

Code 10-24. Save Function for the EditBlogPost Page

```
private async void Save()
{
    blogPost!.Tags = CleanTags(tags.Split(','));

    if (mode == "create")
```

```
    {
        blogPost.PublishedDate = DateTime.Now;
        blogPost =
            await service.Create(blogPost);
    }
    else
    {
        await service.Update(blogPost);
    }

    navigationManager.NavigateTo➡
        ($"blogposts/{blogPost.Author}/{blogPost.Id}");
}
```

When the user clicks save, the first thing that we need to do is split the tags up from a comma-separated string and back into a list of strings. To make life easier for the user, we are cleaning the input before we save it.

If we are in "create" mode, then we set the PublishedDate to DateTime.Now and then save the blog post using the BlogPostService.

The Author and Id fields are not set before we save the blog post as that will be done in the API. We do set the Id with the value returned from the save function so that we can use it for redirecting later in the function.

If we are updating a blog post, then we can simply call the Update function of the BlogPostService.

Finally, after the saving has been completed, we redirect back to the view page for the blog post.

Now we can start displaying the edit form on the page.

8. Add the code snippet from Code 10-25 above the @code block.

Code 10-25. AuthorizeView and EditForm for the EditBlogPost Page

```
<AuthorizeView Roles="admin">
    <Authorized>

    @if (blogPost is null)
    {
        <div>Loading...</div>
    }
```

```
    else
    {
        <EditForm
            Model="blogPost"
            OnValidSubmit="Save"
            Context="EditContext">

        </EditForm>
    }
    </Authorized>
</AuthorizeView>
```

We are wrapping the code for the editing in an AuthorizeView, again to ensure that only users with the admin role can see the edit form.

While we are waiting for the blog post to be loaded, we display a loading text.

Once loaded, we show the EditForm itself. We pass the object being edited, the blogPost and set the function to call when the form is valid and a Submit button is pressed.

Finally, we name the Context of the EditForm to be EditContext. We need to do the last step because both the AuthorizeForm and EditForm have a built-in object called Context, and they will interfere with each other if the naming is left unchanged.

Now we can add the HTML controls for the editing itself.

9.   Add the code snippet from Code 10-26 into the EditForm component on the page.

Code 10-26.   HTML Controls for Editing the BlogPost

```
<div>
    <label>Title</label>
    <div><InputText @bind-Value=blogPost.Title /></div>
</div>
<div>
    <label>Tags</label>
    <div><InputText @bind-Value=tags /></div>
</div>
```

```
<div>
    <label>Post</label>
    <div>
        <InputTextArea
            @bind-Value=blogPost.BlogPostMarkdown
            style=" width: 100%; ➥
            height: 60vh; min-height: 100px;" />
    </div>
</div>
<button type="submit">Save</button>
```

We are adding four controls to the page here:

- The title

- The tags for the blog post

- The blog post itself

- The submit button to save the blog post

The title and tags are just plain input controls. The post itself though is a text area – this allows multiline input and a bigger typing area.

The tags control isn't connected directly to the blogPost object specified in the EditForm, rather it is accessing a private variable for the page. This is because the tags are stored as a list of strings, but here we are allowing users to simply enter a comma-separated list of values in a single string.

We are also adding some styling to the blog post control. This styling will make the control as wide as the screen, and take up 60% of the visible view area, with a minimum height of 100 pixels.

This should be put into a CSS class but is kept inline here for simplicity.

Our create and edit functionality is now complete – the only thing left is to provide access to it from our existing pages!

Adding the Create Link

The create link will be at the top of the blog post list.

1. Open the BlogPostSummaries.razor page.

2. Add the code snippet from Code 10-27 below the H1 tag on the page.

Code 10-27. Create Link for the BlogPosts Page

```
<AuthorizeView Roles="admin">
    <Authorized>
        <a href="blogposts/new/edit">Create</a>
    </Authorized>
</AuthorizeView>
```

This code checks to see if the user has the admin role and, if so, displays the link to the create URL.

Adding the Edit and Delete Links

The Edit and Delete links will be added in the FullBlogPost.razor page.

1. Open the "FullBlogPost.razor" file.

2. Add the code snippet from Code 10-28 to the page under the injection of the BlogPostService.

Code 10-28. NavigationManager Injection

```
@inject NavigationManager navigationManager
```

We will use the NavigationManager to redirect away from the page when we delete a blog post.

Next, we need to add the two links themselves.

1. Add the code snippet from Code 10-29 above the <article> tag displaying the blog post.

Code 10-29. Edit and Delete Links for the FullBlogPost.razor Page

```
<AuthorizeView Roles="admin">
    <Authorized>
        <a href="blogposts/@blogPost.Author➥
            /@blogPost.Id/edit">Edit</a>
        <a href="javascript:;" @onclick="Delete">Delete</a>
    </Authorized>
</AuthorizeView>
```

Again, we are making sure that the user has the correct admin role to see the links. The Edit link simply redirects to the edit page, using the Id of the blog post being viewed.

The Delete functionality is a little more complex. There is an onclick event linking the Delete method that we will write next. But there is also a piece of JavaScript in the href attribute. This JavaScript allows us to set a href property (so that the delete link displays the same as the Edit link) but ensures that the browser does nothing with it when clicked.

Now for the final code. The Delete method itself.

2. Add the code snippet from Code 10-30 under the OnParametersSetAsync function on the page.

Code 10-30. Delete Method for FullBlogPost.razor

```
private async void Delete()
{
    await service.Delete(blogPost!.Id, blogPost!.Author);
    navigationManager.NavigateTo("blogposts");
}
```

This method first calls the delete function on the BlogPostService and then redirects the user back to the full list of blog posts.

Deploy and Test

That's all the code that we need to make the edit functionality in our application.

In the Git Changes pane in Visual Studio, commit the changes and push to GitHub.

Once the site has been deployed, we can log in with the account with the "admin" role, which we set in Chapter 9.

When we browse to the "blog posts" page, we should now see the Create link at the top of the page, as seen in Figure 10-1.

Blog posts

Create

Your First Page

C#, Blazor,

Consectetur adipiscing elit. Mauris suscipit laoreet enim eleifend elementum. Nam tellus urna, sodales sit amet facilisis vel, sollicitudin sed lorem. Donec tincidunt nisl ut molestie ultricies. Pellentesque posuere libero ac aliquam elementum. Class aptent taciti sociosqu ad litora torquent per conubia nostra, per inceptos himenaeos. Donec placerat eget ante ut molestie. Praesent vehicula consequat tortor. Praesent accumsan leo lorem, at finibus turpis semper et. Aliquam varius vehicula purus n

Figure 10-1. *Blog Post Create Link*

When we click the link, we will be redirected to our edit page, with all fields empty. Fill in some text to create a new blog post, as seen in Figure 10-2.

Figure 10-2. *Create Blog Post Page*

Click "save"; we are now redirected to the blog post display page. Here, we can see the two new buttons: edit and delete, as seen in Figure 10-3.

Figure 10-3. *Edit and Delete Functionality in Blog Post Display Page*

When we click "edit," we open the edit page, which looks the same as Figure 10-2. Make a change and then click "save." We return to the blog post display page. If we refresh this page, we can see that the changes are still visible.

If we click delete, the blog post is removed, and we are redirected to the list of blog posts.

We can now create and edit posts!

Conclusion

And with that, the code for our blog application is complete. We have a fully functional application for both users to read blog posts and for us to create and edit new ones.

We've completed the functionality in this book by adding the edit functionality, adding new Azure functions to handle the "POST," "PUT," and "DELETE" HTTP methods we use to create and edit data, then securing those routes using the "staticwebapp. config.json" file so that only "admin" users have access to them.

We've changed the "BlogPostService" in the Client application to use those endpoints and to ensure that our cached data is up to date when we make changes.

Finally, we added a page for creating and editing blog posts and provided access to this functionality in the user interface.

There are many improvements that we can make to our application going forward, see "appendix A" for ideas for self-study, but our coding for the project is complete.

In the remainder of the book, we will look at how we can use the Azure Static Web App, and its Static Web App CLI, to help our developer workflow when working with our application and help us turn our website into our own brand using custom domains.

The source code for this book is available on GitHub, located at `https://github.com/Apress/beginning-azure-static-web-apps`. For the completed code for this chapter, use the "chapter-10" folder.

PART IV

SWA Functionality

At the end of the previous chapter, we were finished with our application. It has all of the functionality that we need to create, update, and delete blog posts and for users to browse those blog posts.

In this final part, we are going to look at some last functionality to make the Azure Static Web App easier to work with.

We will start with a deeper look at how we can use the Azure Static Web App CLI to support our developer inner loop and to allow us to better test our application locally.

We'll then look at how we can test our application in an Azure environment without deploying to production.

And finally, we'll look at adding custom domains to our application to give it an easier-to-remember URL.

CHAPTER 11

Static Web App CLI

We've used the Azure Static Web App CLI (SWA CLI) in an earlier chapter to get started with debugging when running Visual Studio. But there is a lot more that the Static Web App CLI can do!

We are not going to cover everything it can do – but will look at some of the options that can make our developer flow better. We'll run our application without using Visual Studio and run our application from the same static files that are deployed to Azure to ensure that we have our configuration files set up correctly.

We'll look at how the SWA CLI can support our development flow when working with authentication and authorization and finally look at the configuration file that the SWA CLI has available to enable us to simplify how we use the SWA CLI itself.

Technical Requirements

To complete the steps in this chapter, you will need the application from Chapter 10 available and the SWA CLI that we installed in Chapter 5.

The source code for this book is available on GitHub, located at `https://github.com/Apress/beginning-azure-static-web-apps`. For this chapter, use the "chapter-10" folder for the start code.

Running the Application

Back in Chapter 5, we debugged our application by setting both the Client and Api projects to start when we ran our application and then using the default options of the SWA to glue the two together and allow us to use the application locally.

But for those times when we just want to run the application locally rather than debug the code, we can do this via the command line directly.

© Stacy Cashmore 2022
S. Cashmore, *Beginning Azure Static Web Apps*, https://doi.org/10.1007/978-1-4842-8146-8_11

To do this, we are going to use three separate commands to see everything needed to run the application.

1. Open three terminal windows.

2. In the first window, go to the Client folder of our solution and run the command from Code 11-1. This will start the Blazor application.

Code 11-1. Running the Client Application

```
dotnet watch run
```

3. In the second window, go to the Api folder of our solution and run the command from Code 11-2.
   This command will check the code in the folder for Azure Functions and what language has been used to create it.
   It will then compile and run the Azure Functions.

Code 11-2. Func Start Command

```
func start
```

4. In the last terminal window, we can run the SWA CLI itself to join these two together.
   Go to the root folder of the solution (which contains both the Client and Api projects) and run the command from Code 11-3.

Code 11-3. Static Web App CLI Start Command

```
swa start https://localhost:5000
```

This command, the same as we used in Chapter 5, will start the Node.js server that replicates the Azure Static Web App that we have in production.

When running, we can visit `http://localhost:4280` and see our application running without using Visual Studio.

But this is still three terminals, and it's not convenient. Let's improve this!

First, we are going to run the Azure Functions for our API differently, so that we no longer need that terminal.

1. Close the terminal window where we ran the API Azure Functions using "func start."

2. Stop the Static Web App CLI by pressing "Ctrl" + "C".

3. Restart it with the command from Code 11-4.

Code 11-4. Static Web App CLI Start Command with Azure Functions

```
swa start https://localhost:5000 --api-location ./Api
```

This command will run the "func start" command with the contents of the "Api" folder when starting the Node.js server.

Once running, we can see that our application is still running on the same `http://localhost:4280` URL.

Now we'll remove the need to start the Client application separately. This is a little more complex than running the Api inside of the Static Web App CLI.

1. Close the terminal with the "dotnet watch run" command.

2. Stop the Static Web App CLI using "Ctrl" + "C".

3. Restart the Static Web App CLI with the command from Code 11-5.

Code 11-5. Static Web App CLI Start Command with Client and Api

```
swa start https://localhost:5000 --api-location ./Api ➥
    --run "dotnet watch run --project ./Client"
```

We now also include the "dotnet watch run" command when we start the Node.js server. It looks a little different from when we ran it in the terminal though.

Because we start the Static Web App CLI in the root folder for the solution, the run command is also executed with the root folder as the working directory. We add the "--project .\Client" to the command so that the dotnet CLI starts in the correct location to find the code.

Using this command, we can now run the application locally using only one terminal window.

If we visit the `https://localhost:4280` URL, we can see that our application still works.

Remember to check the correct URL; when "dotnet watch run" is executed, it opens a new browser with the Client application not running via the Static Web App CLI. I have made the mistake multiple times of looking at this browser rather than running the Static Web App CLI URL, and then wondering why the code was not working.

The command is a little long and complex – but we will look at improving that later in the chapter!

Changing Port Numbers

Running the Static Web App CLI with the defaults as they come out of the box makes the tool simple for us to use. However, there are times when those default port numbers won't work for us.

Azure Function Port Numbers

We'll start looking at the port numbers used for the Azure Functions.

In our book, we have ensured that our Api project runs on the default port number, 7071. This used to be the default port for an Azure Function when running from both the command line and from Visual Studio.

From the command line, it still is. However, as we saw back in Chapter 5, it no longer is when running from Visual Studio. To make our examples simpler to use, we reverted that by manually changing the Visual Studio project to use the default port (as it made it easier to run our examples).

But there is also a way to override the port used by the Static Web App for the API calls. Not only can this be used for running the Static Web App CLI against Azure Functions running on a different port but is also useful when running multiple Azure Functions locally.

1. Stop the Static Web App from the previous section.

2. Run the command from Code 11-6 in the terminal.

Code 11-6. Static Web App CLI Overriding the Default Api Port

```
swa start https://localhost:5000 --api-location ./Api ➡
    --run "dotnet watch run --project ./Client" ➡
    --api-port 7073
```

The command still starts both the Client and Api projects as before, but now sets the Api to start on port 7073. If we look at the terminal running the Static Web App CLI, we can see that requests for the API are forwarded to this port now.

As we included the "--api-location" parameter, this command will start the Azure Functions itself. It also passes the port number to the Azure Functions Core Tools to start the Azure Functions on the required port.

If we do not specify the API location explicitly, as when running the solution using Visual Studio, it simply uses the port number to know where to send API requests to the application.

Changing the Static Web App CLI Default Port

It can also happen that we need to run the Static Web App CLI itself on a different port. Either if port 4280 is already in use or if you have two Static Web Apps that you are debugging at the same time.

1.   Stop the Static Web App CLI from the previous section.

2.   Run the command from Code 11-7 in the terminal.

Code 11-7. Static Web App CLI Overriding the Default Port

```
swa start https://localhost:5000 --api-location ./Api ➡
    --run "dotnet watch run --project ./Client" ➡
    --port 4281
```

This command starts the application as normal, only now the application is available on 4281. Open `http://localhost:4281` to see the application working.

Changing the Client Port

The final part of our application is the client. However, as we point the SWA CLI to the client application directly when starting the Static Web App CLI, we do not need to override the port number when starting the application. Rather, we would just use a different URL as the location of the Client application to start with.

1.   Stop the Static Web App CLI command from the previous section.

2.   Run the command from Code 11-8.

Code 11-8. Static Web App CLI with Different Client Port Number

```
swa start http://localhost:5001 --api-location ./Api ➡
    --run "dotnet watch run --project ./Client"
```

In this example, we are using the HTTP port associated with our Client application; until now, we have always used the HTTPS port.

Because we point directly at the full URL, we do not need to add anything else to our command.

If we check the `http://localhost:4280` URL, as we have not overridden the Static Web App CLI port, we need to revert to the 4280 port; we can see that the application is still working, only now the requests are directed to the `http://localhost:5001` port.

Running Static Content

When we run our application, either using Visual Studio or via the command line, there is a development server running to serve our files. This works well during development; we can quickly run the application and can debug our code.

However, in our production Azure Static Web App environment, there is no server. We are serving static files to the browser. We've already seen that this can cause different behavior locally vs. in production when a user tries to directly access a page in our application that only exists on the client – something that we handle using the "navigationFallback" property of the "staticwebapp.config.json" file.

Because of this, it can be useful to run our application locally also using these static files, avoiding both Visual Studio and the dotnet CLI at runtime.

Publish the Client Project

The first step in running our application locally using static files is to publish the Client project. This will compile the project and create the same static files that we will use in production locally. These can then be served without the .NET development server.

1. Stop the Static Web App CLI from the previous section.

2. Run the command from Code 11-9.

Code 11-9. Dotnet Publish Command

```
dotnet publish ./Client/Client.csproj --output ./dist
```

These files will be generated in the "dist/wwwroot" folder in the root folder of the solution.

Run the Static Web App CLI with Static Files

Now we can use these static files to run the full application.

1. Stop the Static Web App CLI from the previous section.

2. Run the code from Code 11-10 in the root folder of the solution.

Code 11-10. Static Web App CLI Using Static Files

```
swa start ./dist/wwwroot --api-location ./Api
```

Running this command doesn't start the compilation of the Client project, as we have previously used. Instead, we now get a message telling us that the Static Web App CLI is serving static content from the "./dist/wwwroot" folder, as seen in Code 11-11.

Code 11-11. Example Static Web App CLI Output Showing Static Content Being Served

```
[swa]
[swa] Serving static content:
[swa]    C:\github\beginning-static-web-apps\dist\wwwroot
[swa]
```

When we open the app now, there are two main differences:

- The application should run faster because the published static files are optimized for delivery to the browser.

- Because there is no development server behind the static files that we are serving, we can test that our navigation fallback is working correctly.

While we don't need to use this method of running our application every time we deploy, it's good to know how to run the application in this way.

Extending the .gitignore File

When we publish the Client project, we create a lot of new files. By default, these would be added to our GitHub repo, something that we don't want.

Over the course of our journey, we have had other files added to our solution when using Visual Studio; these haven't been added to our GitHub repo because of the ".gitignore" file that we added when the repo was created. We are going to expand this so that our published files are also ignored.

While we are using Visual Studio for developing our code, for these files (and other non-.NET development) Visual Studio Code is a better option for this step.

1. Stop the Static Web App CLI from the previous section.

2. Open Visual Studio Code using the command from Code 11-12.
   This will open the current folder with Visual Studio Code.

Code 11-12. Opening Visual Studio Code

code .

3. Check how many files are currently classed as modified by Git; see Figure 11-1 as an example with 295 changes.

Figure 11-1. *Git Icon Showing Modified Files in Visual Studio Code*

4. Open the ".gitignore" file, seen in Figure 11-2.

Figure 11-2. *Visual Studio Code File Explorer*

5. Add the line from Code 11-13 to the end of the file.

    This rule tells Git to ignore any files and folders in the "dist" folder. Any files added here, or altered here, will therefore not be included when we next commit changes.

Code 11-13. .gitignore Rule for Published Client Project

```
dist/
```

6. Save the file so that it takes effect.
    We should see that we now have one change – the .gitignore file itself.

7. Exit Visual Studio Code.

Static Web App CLI Configuration

Now that we can see the different ways that we can run our application using the Static Web App CLI, let's look at how we can make it easier to use for our main use cases.

To do this, we are going to use a configuration file to allow us to run one or more predefined scenarios with simplified commands. We are going to set up three commands for our solution:

- Debugging the application using Visual Studio

- Running the application from the command line

- Running the application using the static published files

The Azure Static Web App CLI can also work with a configuration file, where we can create one or more profiles for how it should run.

1. Open Visual Studio Code as we did in the last section.

2. Click the new file icon in the file explorer, shown in Figure 11-3.

Figure 11-3. *New File Icon in Visual Studio Code*

3. Name the file "swa-cli.config.json"; the file should automatically open.

4. Paste the code from Code 11-14 into the new file.

Code 11-14. Static Web App CLI Configuration JSON

```json
{
    "configurations": {
        "static": {
            "appLocation": "./dist/wwwroot",
            "apiLocation": "./Api"
        },
        "run-all": {
            "appDevserverUrl": "https://localhost:5000",
            "apiLocation": "./Api",
            "run": "dotnet watch run --project ./Client"
        },
        "debug": {
            "appDevserverUrl": "https://localhost:5000"
```

```
        }
    }
}
```

5. Save the file.

6. Exit Visual Studio Code.

This configuration gives us access to three different ways of running our application from the command line:

- "static" runs the site using the static files that we have just created in the "/dist" folder and runs the Api project from the "./Api" folder.

- "run-all" runs the .NET development server for the Client application and runs the Api project from the "./Api" folder.

- "debug" connects the Static Web App CLI to the Client development server, and the Api, running already. This allows us to connect to the Visual Studio application.

Each configuration takes the command-line arguments we used previously and uses them as properties of the configuration object.

There are some differences though. On the command line, we can use the location of the published files and the URL of the development server interchangeably. When using the configuration, we need to explicitly state whether we are linking to a file location or development server.

Let's try our new configuration file to see how it works.

First, we are going to test the "debug" configuration.

1. Open Visual Studio and run both the Client and Api projects.

2. In the terminal, run the command from Code 11-15.

Code 11-15. Static Web App CLI Using the "debug" Configuration

```
swa start debug
```

When the Static Web App CLI starts, we can see that it picks up that we are using a configuration setting from our file; see Code 11-16.

Code 11-16.   Static Web App CLI Output Snippet for Configuration

```
Welcome to Azure Static Web Apps CLI (1.0.1)

Using configuration "debug" from file:
  C:\github\beginning-static-web-apps\swa-cli.config.json
```

    3. Open `http://localhost:4280` in a browser and check that it is working.

Next up, we'll try the "run-all" option.

    1. Stop the Static Web App CLI from the previous example.

    2. Stop the Client and Api projects inside of Visual Studio.

    3. At the terminal, run the command from Code 11-17.

Code 11-17.   Static Web App CLI Using the "run-all" Configuration

```
swa start run-all
```

As we can see in the terminal, it is now using the "run-all" configuration and has started both the Client and Api projects.

    4. Open `http://localhost:4280` in a browser and check that it is working.

Finally, we will test the "static" option.

    1. Stop the Static Web App CLI from the previous example.

    2. Publish the application again as we did previously.

    3. Run the command from Code 11-17.

In a terminal, run the command from Code 11-18.

Code 11-18.   Static Web App CLI Using the "static" Option

```
swa start static
```

We can now see that the static configuration option has been used, and we are serving the content of the "./dist/wwwroot" folder.

    4. Open `http://localhost:4280` in a browser and check that it is working.

Commit Our Changes

While we haven't made any code changes in this chapter, we do need to commit the configuration changes that we have made.

Open Visual Studio and commit and push the changes that we have made. If the ".gitignore" has been updated successfully, we should only see two files in the list of changes:

- .gitignore

- swa-cli.config.json

Now that these files are on GitHub, anyone who we allow access to our repository can run the same three commands that we have just used to run the application locally.

Conclusion

Over this chapter, we have looked at how the SWA CLI can help us in our developer inner loop. From running the application outside of Visual Studio to running the application as it will be deployed.

We've looked at how we can run multiple applications side by side locally without interfering with each other.

Finally, we have set up a configuration file so that we can easily run our application using simple commands.

We've only scratched the surface of what the SWA CLI, and associated configurations, can do for us – but what we have used can dramatically simplify our development workflow and allow us to have a better idea how our application is going to work in a production environment.

In our next chapter, we'll look at how we can check how our application works in a production-like environment in Azure itself using the built-in staging environments and pull request functionality inside of GitHub.

The source code for this book is available on GitHub, located at `https://github.com/Apress/beginning-azure-static-web-apps`. For the completed code for this chapter, see the "chapter-11" folder.

CHAPTER 12

Testing in Azure

In the previous chapter, we looked at how we can improve our development flow locally. By using the Static Web App CLI, we could replicate the functionality found in Azure Static Web Apps on the command line. To ensure that we could also check how our published application was going to run, we also looked at how to use the published files.

However, this does not ensure that our application is going to run the same way inside of the Azure resource itself. As the Static Web App CLI itself says, there could be differences.

In this chapter, we are going to look at the last stage of deploying new functionality to production. That is testing in Azure itself.

We will look at the GitHub workflow in a little more detail, make a change, and see it running in Azure before we move it to production.

And we'll look at the limitations that we have when using this functionality.

Technical Requirements

To complete the steps in this chapter, you will need to have the Azure Account created in Chapter 2, a deployed Azure Static Web App from Chapter 4, and the application from Chapter 11 available in a GitHub repository.

The source code for this book is available on GitHub, located at `https://github.com/Apress/beginning-azure-static-web-apps`. For this chapter, use the "chapter-11" folder for the start code.

Azure Static Web App Staging Slots

To test in Azure, without testing in our production environment, we need a separate Azure Static Web App that we can deploy into. Thankfully, Azure Static Web Apps can manage these automatically for us.

© Stacy Cashmore 2022
S. Cashmore, *Beginning Azure Static Web Apps*, https://doi.org/10.1007/978-1-4842-8146-8_12

This happens automatically whenever we create a pull request from a development branch into our main branch and is handled in the same workflow file that deploys our application each time we've made a change to our application.

Open the workflow file in GitHub. You can find this in the ".github/workflows/" folder of the repository.

At the top of the file, there is a section labeled "pull_request"; see Code 12-1.

Code 12-1. Pull Request Section of GitHub Workflow File

```
pull_request:
  types: [opened, synchronize, reopened, closed]
  branches:
    - main
```

This section will ensure that the workflow file is triggered whenever there is a pull request opened, synchronized, reopened, or closed against the main branch.

In the "build_and_deploy_job," there is a check to ensure that the job is run not only when a change is made to the main branch but also whenever a pull request triggers the workflow, and it is not being closed. See Code 12-2.

Code 12-2. Build and Deploy Job Control

```
build_and_deploy_job:
  if: github.event_name == 'push' || (github.event_name == ➡
    'pull_request' && github.event.action != 'closed')
```

The build job works differently for a pull request though. When we push a change to our main branch, it is built and deployed to our production environments, as we have seen throughout the book.

When we build a pull request, an entirely new staging environment is created. The code from the pull request is built and deployed into the new environment and a comment linking to the environment is left on the pull request itself.

Making a Branch

Let's make some changes to our application using pull requests to see this in action!

1. Open the solution in Visual Studio.

2. Open the git changes window.

3. Open the branch drop-down box, as shown in Figure 12-1.

Figure 12-1. *Git Branch Selection*

4. Click the "New Branch" button visible in Figure 12-1.

5. In the screen that opens, fill in the name of a branch, and for "Based on:" select the main branch as shown in Figure 12-2.

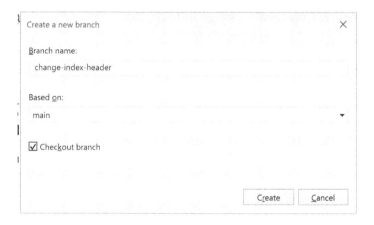

Figure 12-2. *Create a New Branch Window*

6. Click "Create" to create and switch to the new branch.

Now that we have our branch, we just need to make some changes to push to GitHub for our pull request.

To do this, we'll make a change to our "Index.razor" page.

1. In the Client project, in the "Pages" folder open the "Index. razor" file.

2. Update the "<PageTitle>" contents to something that better describes the application.

Save the change, commit the file, and push the change to GitHub.

Creating the Staging Slot

To create the staging slot, we first need to create a pull request in GitHub.

1. Open the GitHub repository in a browser.

We can see the message that there has been a change in a branch; see Figure 12-3.

Figure 12-3. *Branch Changed Message in GitHub*

2. Click the "Compare and pull request" button.

3. On the pull request page, as seen in Figure 12-4, enter a title and description of the change.

Open a pull request

Create a new pull request by comparing changes across two branches. If you need to, you can also compare across forks.

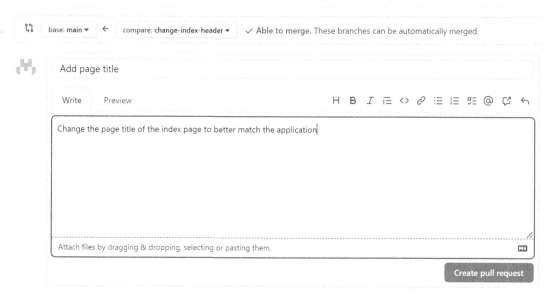

Figure 12-4. *GitHub Pull Request Creation Page*

4.   Click the "Create" button.

5.   In the page that opens, we will see after a few seconds that a workflow starts; see Figure 12-5.

Figure 12-5. *GitHub Pull Request Workflow*

Once the workflow has finished, the outline will change from orange to green.

Testing in the Cloud

A couple of seconds after the workflow has finished running, we'll get a comment on our pull request with a link to our staging environment; see Figure 12-6.

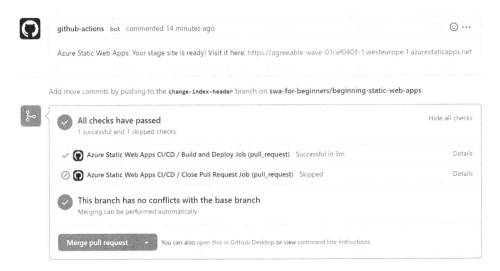

Figure 12-6. *Link to Staging Environment in the GitHub Pull Request*

1. Open the link in a new browser tab.

If we look at the URL, we can see that it looks similar, but not the same as the normal URL for the production Azure Static Web App:

```
<base-url>-<pull-request-number>.<azure-swa-region>.<number>.
azurestaticapps.net
```

This means that every time we make a pull request, it will get its own unique URL that we can use for testing.

If we look at the title of the page in the browser tab, we should see the change that we made in our code. See Figure 12-7 for a comparison to the live site which is unchanged.

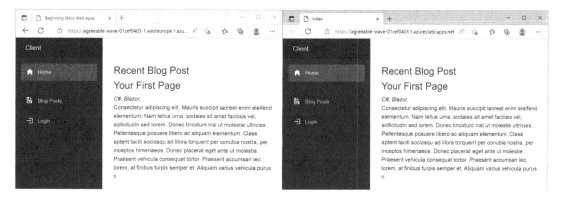

Figure 12-7. *Staging Environment Browser Tab Name*

Making a Second Change

This is great, but what happens when we spot an error in the staging environment or see an extra change that we need to make? Let's try that now by making a second change.

We changed the title of the browser tab, but maybe we should also put something on the screen so that it really stands out to our users.

1. In the Client project, in the "Pages" folder, open the "Index.razor" page again.

2. Under the "<PageTitle>" tag we added previously, add the code snippet from Code 12-3.

Code 12-3. Index.razor

```
<h1>Beginning Static Web Apps</h1>
```

Ensure that the branch for the change is selected, commit the change, and push it again to GitHub.

Revisiting the Stage Environment

If we look at the pull request in GitHub now, we should see that the same workflow that was triggered when we created our pull request has been retriggered; see Figure 12-8.

Add more commits by pushing to the `change-index-header` branch on swa-for-beginners/beginning-static-web-apps.

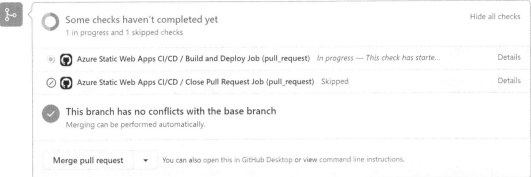

Figure 12-8. *GitHub Pull Request*

Just as our main branch is built and deployed on every change, the pull request code will also be built and redeployed each time our new branch is updated.

Once the workflow has finished, reopen the pull request URL and check that the change made is visible on the index page.

Staging Environment Settings

There is one problem with our staging environment right now: it is using the same environment settings as our production environment. This means that we can do a like-for-like comparison with our application when comparing it to a production environment.

But it also means that if we change any data, we'll be changing production data for tests. Not great.

For a full application, we would have a different set of database connection strings for production, testing, and development work to ensure that this data isn't shared between environments.

To support this, we can return the configuration settings of our Azure Static Web App.

Once a staging environment is available, we can use the drop-down menu shown in Figure 12-9.

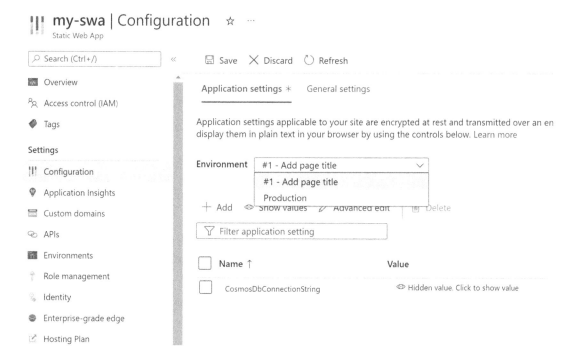

Figure 12-9. *Environment Selection for Configurations*

If we select the staging environment, we can see that the values for the staging environment are automatically copied from the production environment when it is created.

But once it has been created, we can change those values so that the environment can use different resources.

We are not going to do this for our application, but it is good to know that the functionality exists.

Staging Environment Limitations

While the staging environments that we have available to us are amazing, they have some limitations.

The first one to mention is based on the staging environment configuration options we've just looked at. While each staging environment can have its own configuration, it needs to be set up after the environment has been created.

There are ways to work around this shortcoming, by using development, release, and production branches. But those concepts are out of scope for this book.

Free Tier

In our demonstration, we are using the free tier of Azure Static Web Apps. This is great for hobby projects or getting started. But there are, of course, limitations. Staging environments are one of these.

There are two limitations that we need to deal with.

Number of Staging Slots

At the time of writing, we can only have three staging environments per Azure Static Web App.

This effectively limits the amount of active pull requests we can do at any one time to three. For a hobby project, that is not a problem, but for larger projects, it may be a limiting factor to be considered.

If needed, a Standard Tier Azure Static Web App can be used which increases this quota of staging environments to ten.

Public Access to Staging Slot

On the free tier, the staging slots are available publicly. If someone enters the URL, they will be able to see the changes that are being tested.

Again, for hobby sites, this may not be a problem. However, for projects that require changes to be private until they are released to the public, using these free tier staging slots isn't going to be a possibility.

In this case, there are two options.

We can either remove the pull request triggers in the workflow file. This will ensure that our workflow does not start when a pull request is started.

The other option is to use a standard tier Azure Static Web App. When we do this, we can ensure that a password is needed to access the staging slot, keeping it more secure.

Removing Staging Environments

We've seen how a staging environment is created and used and what the limitations of those environments are. One of those mentioned was the number of staging environments that we have available. This means that we also need to clean up these staging environments when we no longer need them.

Automatically Cleaning Staging Environments

This is also achieved using the workflow file that we have looked at.

If we look at the second job in our workflow file, as seen in Code 12-4, we can see how the staging environments are cleaned up.

Code 12-4. Close Pull Request Job from Workflow File

```
close_pull_request_job:
    if: github.event_name == 'pull_request' && ➥
     github.event.action == 'closed'
    runs-on: ubuntu-18.04
    name: Close Pull Request Job
    steps:
      - name: Close Pull Request
        id: closepullrequest
        uses: Azure/static-web-apps-deploy@v1
        with:
          azure_static_web_apps_api_token: ${{ ➥
              secrets.AZURE_STATIC_WEB_APPS_API_TOKEN_GREEN_RIVER➥
              _00413E103 }}
          action: "close"
```

We can see in the job that this one only runs for pull requests, and only when they are closed, as mentioned in the job name and description.

It uses the same action as the build and deploy job, only now it is called with a "close" action. This action cleans up the staging environment that was created inside of Azure for our pull request.

Let's close the pull request that we have open.

1.   Open the pull request we just created.

We have two options. We can just use the "Close pull request" button. In which case our staging environment will be removed, but the code will not be merged into the main branch and deployed to production.

Or we can merge the pull request. In which case the code changes that we have made will be merged to the main branch – triggering a separate workflow run to deploy those changes to production and also performing the cleanup.

In Figure 12-10, we can see the two buttons: "Merge" and "Close pull request."

Add more commits by pushing to the **change-index-header** branch on **swa-for-beginners/beginning-static-web-apps**.

All checks have passed
1 successful and 1 skipped checks

Hide all checks

✓ Azure Static Web Apps CI/CD / Build and Deploy Job (pull_request)   Successful in 3m   Details

⊘ Azure Static Web Apps CI/CD / Close Pull Request Job (pull_request)   Skipped   Details

This branch has no conflicts with the base branch
Merging can be performed automatically.

Merge pull request ▾   You can also open this in GitHub Desktop or view command line instructions.

Write   Preview   H B 𝐼 ≔ <> 𝒫 ≔ ≔ ≝ @ ↗ ↩

Leave a comment

Attach files by dragging & dropping, selecting or pasting them.

⇅ Close pull request   Comment

***Figure 12-10.** Merge and Close Options in GitHub Pull Request*

We are going to put our changes to production today.

2.   Click "Merge pull request" and then "Confirm merge."

Now when we look at the actions in GitHub, we can see two workflows running, as we see in Figure 12-11.

● Merge pull request #1 from swa-for-beginners/change-in...
Azure Static Web Apps CI/CD #13: Commit f5dfd8e pushed by swa-for-
beginners   main   🗂 now   ⏱ Queued   ...

● Add page title
Azure Static Web Apps CI/CD #12: Pull request #1 closed by swa-for-beginners   change-index-header   🗂 now   ⏱ Queued   ...

***Figure 12-11.** GitHub Actions Running After Closing the Pull Request*

Manually Cleaning Up Environments

If we have too many staging environments, or if the workflow for removing a staging environment fails for any reason, we can remove the staging environment manually.

If we open the Azure Portal for the Azure Static Web App and go to the Environments screen, we can see each of the environments that are currently provisioned. See Figure 12-12.

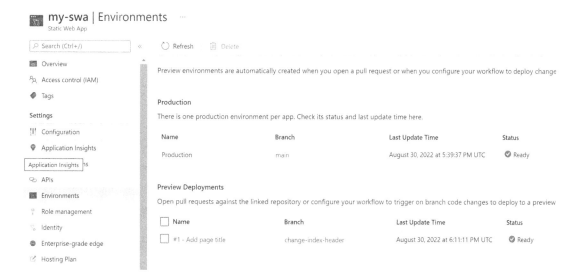

Figure 12-12. *Azure Static Web App Environments Screen*

If we select a staging environment, we can then manually delete it using the "delete" button visible in Figure 12-12. This will free up a slot inside of our application.

If the environment is needed in the future, for an ongoing pull request, for example, we can rerun the action linked in the pull request and recreate the environment.

Conclusion

We can use the built-in staging environments to easily check that our application runs as well in the real Azure resource in the cloud as it does locally when using the Static Web App CLI.

We've looked at creating pull requests for changes and the workflow file associated with it.

We've seen how those environments differ from our production environment and discussed the limitations that we have when using them.

We are almost at the end of our journey. There is only one thing left to look at – the URL we have right now is not very user-friendly! In our last chapter, we will fix that.

The source code for this book is available on GitHub, located at `https://github.com/Apress/beginning-azure-static-web-apps`. For the completed code for this chapter, see the "chapter-12" folder.

CHAPTER 13

Custom Domains

We've reached the last stop in our journey. We have an application that we can build on now. We can create, edit, and delete blog posts.

There is however still one thing that we need to do to make our users' life easier. Our domain name. While the domain names that Azure Static Web Apps create with the resource are fun and unique, they are neither easy to say nor remember.

We need a domain name that better fits our application.

In this chapter, we will look at two ways of adding a custom domain to our application. We'll use an externally managed domain and look at how to use Azure DNS.

At the end of this chapter, our blog application will have a URL that is much simpler to remember!

Technical Requirements

To complete the steps in this chapter, you will need to have the Azure Account created in Chapter 2 and a deployed Azure Static Web App from Chapter 4.

To complete the external domain section of the chapter, access is needed to the DNS records of a chosen domain.

To complete the steps, an externally hosted domain and a domain managed with Azure DNS are required.

The source code for this book is available on GitHub via the book's product page, located at `https://github.com/Apress/beginning-azure-static-web-apps`. For this chapter, see the "chapter-12" folder for the start code.

© Stacy Cashmore 2022
S. Cashmore, *Beginning Azure Static Web Apps*, https://doi.org/10.1007/978-1-4842-8146-8_13

Adding a Custom Domain

There are two ways to add a custom domain to an Azure Static Web App. We can either add a domain that we manage ourselves, or we can add a domain that we manage inside of Azure.

To use either of these routes, there are changes that we need to make to our domains before we start the process. Because these processes can be different depending on where your domains are managed, we are not covering making the changes.

Rather, we will look at how to set up the Azure Static Web App itself.

What Domains to Add

The title of the chapter references a single domain. We may need to use more than one custom domain though depending on what domain we want to use.

Thankfully, a free tier Azure Static Web App can have two custom domains.

If our blog post application is going to be a subdomain of a site, then we can use one custom domain.

For example, if we already have a site on the domain "beginningazurestaticwebapps. dev" and we want to host our application on the subdomain of "blog. beginningazurestaticwebapps.dev," then one custom domain is enough.

If we want the application to be hosted at the apex level though, "beginningazurestaticwebapps.dev," then we are going to need both available custom domains in the free tier.

The reason is that when using an apex domain, users are likely to access our application in two different ways:

- "beginningazurestaticwebapps.dev"

- "www.beginningazurestaticwebapps.dev"

We take it for granted as visitors that these two URLs will probably go to the same place, but technically they do not.

We are going to use an apex domain as our example, so setting up both.

If only the subdomain is needed, for example, "blog.beginningazurestaticwebapps. dev," follow the instructions for "www.beginningazurestaticwebapps.dev".

Azure Portal Custom Domain Pane

For both self-managed and Azure controlled domains, the process of creating a custom domain is started in the same way.

1. Open the Azure Portal and go to the Azure Static Web App resource.

2. On the left-hand side, select Custom Domains; see Figure 13-1.

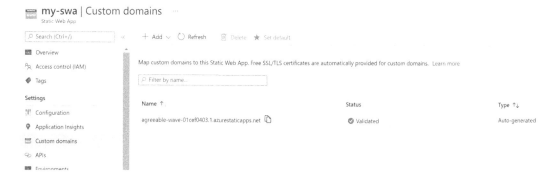

Figure 13-1. *Custom Domain Pane of Azure Static Web Apps*

In this screen, we can see the custom domains available for our application. By default, there is one domain always available – the one created by the Azure Portal itself when we created our Azure Static Web App. This does not count toward our quota of two custom domains.

3. Click the add button, shown in Figure 13-1, to see the two options available to us, as seen in Figure 13-2.

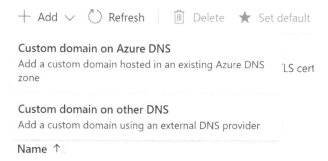

Figure 13-2. *The Add Button for Custom Domains*

Clicking this button gives us access to both the routes for adding a custom domain.

Self-Managed Domain

1. To add a self-managed domain, click the "Custom domain on other DNS," shown in Figure 13-2.

This link opens a slide-in pane on the right-hand side of the pane.

First, we need to enter the domain that we want to enter. Enter the apex domain that you want to enter, for our example: "beginningazurestaticwebapps.dev". See Figure 13-3 for reference.

2. Enter the domain name.

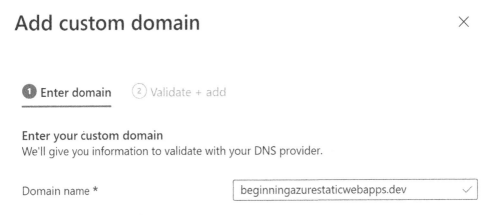

Figure 13-3. *Apex Domain Step 1*

3. Click the Next button.

On the next panel, we get instructions on how to set up our domain.

4. Click the Generate code button, shown in Figure 13-4.

Generate and copy the TXT hostname record and enter it with your DNS provider to confirm your domain ownership. It can take up to 12 hours for DNS entry changes to take effect.

Type	Host	Value	Status
TXT	@	Generate code	

Figure 13-4. *Generate Code Button*

Set up the DNS records of the domain as per the instructions given. For the apex domain, we need to create a "TXT" record for the host "@" with the value generated for us. See Figure 13-5.

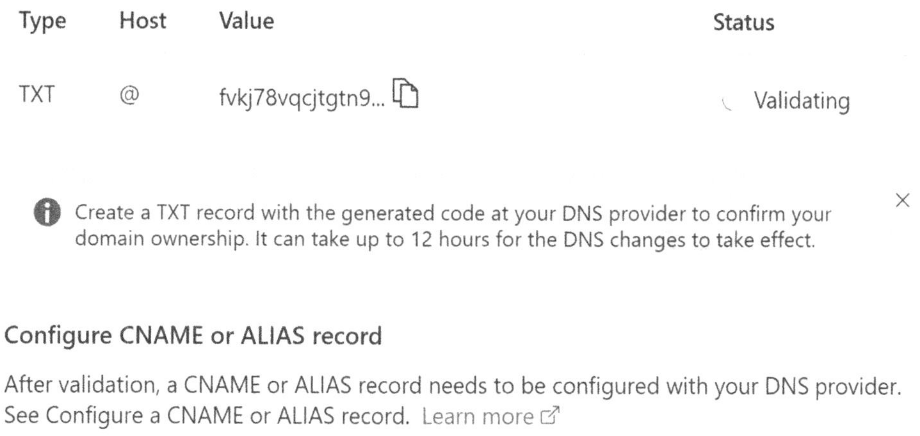

Type	Host	Value	Status
TXT	@	fvkj78vqcjtgtn9... 🗋	Validating

> ℹ Create a TXT record with the generated code at your DNS provider to confirm your ✕
> domain ownership. It can take up to 12 hours for the DNS changes to take effect.

Configure CNAME or ALIAS record

After validation, a CNAME or ALIAS record needs to be configured with your DNS provider. See Configure a CNAME or ALIAS record. Learn more ↗

Figure 13-5. *Add Custom Domain Instructions*

5. Once the DNS records have been created, click "Close."

    The Azure Portal will now check that the correct records exist on the domain.

Now we need to add the "www" variant.
The process is almost the same.

1. Click the "Add" button and select "Custom domain on other DNS."

2. Fill in the "www" variant of the domain in the text box and click "Next."

In the instructions, we can see that we need to add a "CNAME" record for the "www" host with the value given on the panel. See Figure 13-6.

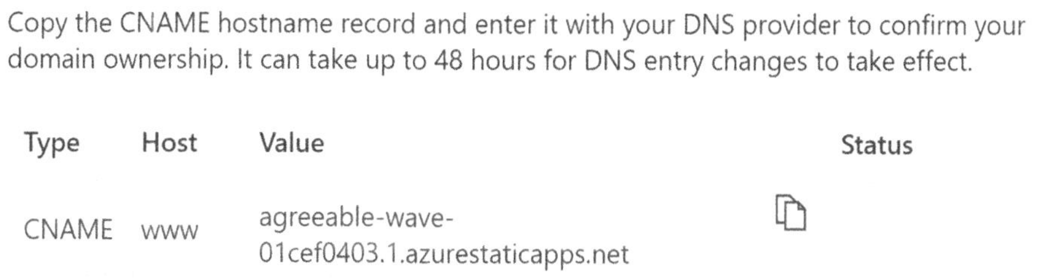

Copy the CNAME hostname record and enter it with your DNS provider to confirm your domain ownership. It can take up to 48 hours for DNS entry changes to take effect.

Type	Host	Value	Status
CNAME	www	agreeable-wave-01cef0403.1.azurestaticapps.net 🗋	

Figure 13-6. *Add WWW Variant of Custom Domain*

3. Once the domain records have been updated, click Add.

Depending on how long it takes for the DNS records to propagate on the Internet, this process can take seconds or hours.

Once finished, return to the "Overview" panel of the Azure Static Web App. If we look at the URL of the application, it no longer shows the Azure-generated URL of the website, but rather the custom domain that we have just entered.

If we visit the site on either the apex or www domain now, we should see our application.

Domain on Azure DNS

When using an Azure DNS Zone, the procedure is somewhat simplified as the Azure Static Web App itself will work out which of the two record types are needed and automatically add them to the DNS Zone.

While there is work in setting up the DNS Zone itself, once available the custom domain itself is simpler to set up.

1. Click "Custom Domain on Azure DNS," shown in Figure 13-2.

2. Enter one of the custom domains (either the apex or the "www").

3. Select the DNS Zone from the drop-down list.

4. When the form is correctly filled, click the apply button; see Figure 13-7.

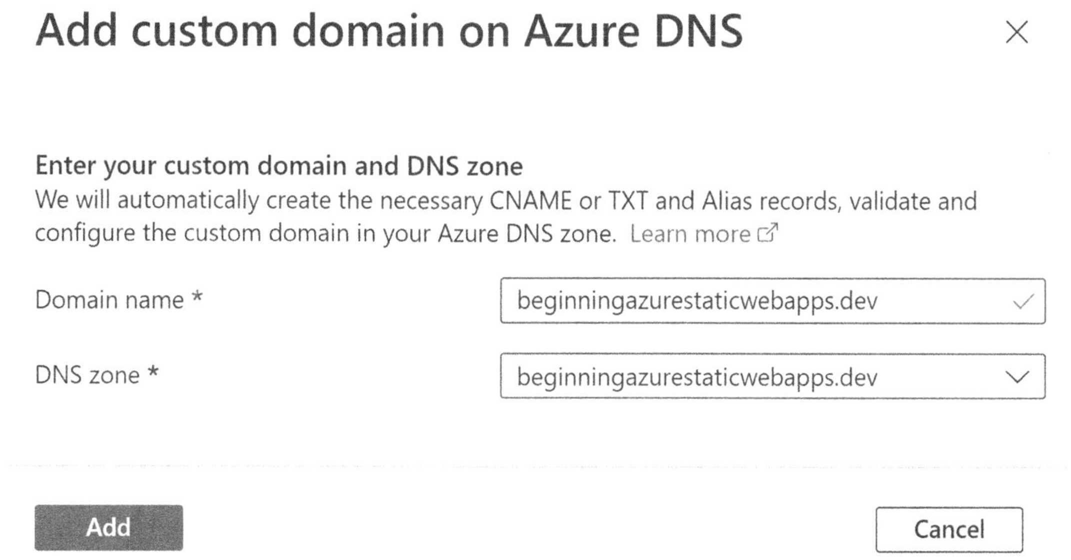

Add custom domain on Azure DNS   ✕

Enter your custom domain and DNS zone
We will automatically create the necessary CNAME or TXT and Alias records, validate and
configure the custom domain in your Azure DNS zone. Learn more ☐

Domain name *	beginningazurestaticwebapps.dev ✓
DNS zone *	beginningazurestaticwebapps.dev ⌄

[**Add**]   [Cancel]

Figure 13-7. *Domain on Azure DNS Filled In*

The Azure Portal will now create the correct records in the Azure DNS Zone. This can be quick, but can also take more than ten minutes to complete.

In the preceding instructions, it was said that either the apex domain or "www" domain could be used, rather than saying to use one or the other – as we did with the DNS domains from the self-hosted DNS instructions. That is because when using Azure DNS, it is the same process for each one.

Once the custom domain has been added, add the second custom domain in the same way.

Once the second domain has been added, we should be able to open the custom domain and see our site working.

Azure-Generated URL

While we now have multiple ways to add custom domains to our application, it's important to know that this does not stop the original URL from still being active.

If we take the original URL from the custom domain panel and visit the site, we can see that it still works.

Also, when a staging environment is created, it also uses the original URL as the base for the URL used by the environment, not a domain based on our new custom domain.

Conclusion

And here we are at the end of our journey together.

We now have a functional blog application where we can create, edit, read, and delete blog posts. We have our inner workflow for developing new functionality and can test these in production as well.

And now our website has an easy-to-say, easy-to-remember URL.

Of course, there is much more that we can do with our application – from the look and feel to extra functionality to make both our life creating posts and our user's life reading content better.

In Appendix A there are some more projects that you can complete to make the application your own using the excellent documentation available to us at aka.ms/swa.

Thank you for allowing me to take this journey with you. I hope that you have enjoyed this journey and can see the possibilities that Azure Static Web Apps can give to us!

The source code for this book is available on GitHub, located at `https://github.com/Apress/beginning-azure-static-web-apps`. For the completed code for this chapter, see the "chapter-12" branch.

Next Steps

We've completed our journey looking into Azure Static Web Apps. The application, however, can still be improved! Here are some ideas for you to implement.

Add User Details

The way that we store the author for a blog post is limited. To keep the application simple, we simply store, and display, the user details of the author. Not only is this not really useful, if the user authenticates with Azure Active Directory or Google, their email address will be displayed with the post. Not ideal for security either.

It would be better if we allowed a user to edit their details in the application. Make a page that allows users to link a display name to their user id.

Then use this display name when we store a new blog post.

This is going to need a new screen in the application, a new shared model, a new object stored in the CosmosDB, and new Azure Functions to create, read, and update the data.

The function for creating blog posts also needs to be updated to get the correct information about the author before storing the blog post.

Blog Post Summary Refresh

We only load the blog post summaries on the first visit to the blog post page where we display the summaries.

To refresh this list, we currently refresh the whole application. It would be better for our users if we could just refresh the list of blog posts themselves.

Add a button for the users to force a refresh of the list of summaries, changing the BlogPostSummaryService to allow this.

© Stacy Cashmore 2022
S. Cashmore, *Beginning Azure Static Web Apps*, https://doi.org/10.1007/978-1-4842-8146-8

Search

When there are not many posts to display, it's easy for users to have an overview of what they are doing. But as the list grows, it gets harder to navigate.

What would help the users is some simple search functionality – on tags and the author level.

The page displaying the post summaries will need changing to allow users to select the tags/authors they wish to see. And the list of blog posts needs to be filtered as these are selected.

With the functionality as it is in the book, this can all be implemented on the Client (as we have a complete list of blog posts). But this challenge can also be taken further by reducing the data needed and only displaying a small number of blog posts at one time, which will mean that both paging and filtering need to be applied to the Azure Function as well.

Custom Summary Length

Our blog post summary length is currently set to 500 characters. But maybe some users would like a longer summary, and some a shorter one.

Also, this number is repeated throughout the application – which means that changing it is harder than it should be.

Expand the user details to include a setting for the length of summary that the user would like. Make sure that if it is not set, we have a default value.

This value will need to be passed to the Azure Function when we retrieve the blog posts.

Preview Complete Flag

A data field that we have in the application is the "PreviewComplete" flag. This indicates that the blog post is a short text. Now it is ignored, but it could be used to both indicate to the user that navigating to the full blog post page isn't needed and to stop the application making calls to the API for the full blog post when it's not needed.

It can also be used to stop the application from loading more data than it needs to. When a full blog post is opened, a check can be made to see if we need to do the round trip to the API.

Tag Lookup

When writing or editing a blog post, we can add tags to help the user understand the contents of the post.

This is a free text entry – so as we need a new tag, we can create one. But to make the process easier, it would also be useful to have a list of tags previously used, either as a lookup field or even something that shows suggestions as we type the tag.

If you have already implemented the search functionality, then you should already have a complete list of tags that you can reuse.

Blog Post Preview

We edit blog posts using Markdown. This makes writing, and storing, our blog posts simple. When we want to display the post, we convert it into HTML.

But wouldn't it be useful to have a preview of our post as we write it?

There are two options for this challenge!

This can either be as simple as a button that displays a preview at that time or as complex as a preview that updates as you enter the text.

Make the Application Multiauthor

Our application right now allows anyone with full rights to edit all blog posts, whether they are the original author or not.

But we have the information available to allow us, for users who are logged in, to ensure that they can only edit their own blog posts.

By implementing this change, we can remove the admin role requirement for the creation, editing, and deletion of posts. All users should be able to make their own posts.

We need to give users their own dashboard to see only their posts.

Fully Implement Post Status

In our CosmosDB queries to select the blog posts that we want to display, we include a clause to ensure that the status is 2. This indicates that the blog post has been published.

This status can be expanded so that we can add draft posts or allow for "soft" deletion of posts.

New parameters will be needed when fetching the blog posts to make this work, and users will need to be able to filter on what they are looking for.

Remember that users should only be able to fill in those details if they have the correct level of rights in the system! Standard users should not see draft or deleted posts that do not belong to them!

Styling

Throughout the book, we have only used the standard styling that we get with Blazor out of the box. It doesn't look bad, but it can look much better!

By using extra styling rules, take the website that we have built together and make it your own!

To complete this, you will need to change the CSS for the application and, optionally, change the structure of the application.

APPENDIX B

Changing the GitHub Workflow

If you have created your Azure Static Web App and the initial deploy failed because the workflow couldn't find the code to deploy, then there is a chance that the Client and Api locations have been set incorrectly.

Opening the Workflow File

We can change the workflow inside of GitHub and ensure that the code is coming from the correct place.

1. Open the GitHub repository in a browser.

2. Click the link to the workflow folder, as seen in Figure B-1.

| | .github/workflows | ci: add Azure Static Web Apps workflow file |
| | Api | Add edit functionality |

Figure B-1. *GitHub Workflow File Location*

3. Click on the workflow file. For a new Azure Static Web App there should only be one file in this folder, see Figure B-2.

| azure-static-web-apps-delightful-field-0f99a2510.yml | ci: add Azure Static Web Apps workflow file |

Figure B-2. *GitHub Workflow File Example*

© Stacy Cashmore 2022
S. Cashmore, *Beginning Azure Static Web Apps*, https://doi.org/10.1007/978-1-4842-8146-8

4. To edit the file, click the pen icon, seen in Figure B-3.

Figure B-3. *GitHub Edit Icon*

5. Ensure that the app_location is pointing to the folder where the Client project is stored.

6. Ensure that the api_location is pointing to the folder where the Api project is stored.

7. Ensure that the output_location is set to the default "wwwroot".

   See Code B-1 for an example configuration.

Code B-1. Example Configuration for app_location, api_location, and output_location

```
app_location: "Client"
api_location: "Api"
output_location: "wwwroot"
```

8. Save the file by clicking "Start commit."

9. In the pop-up that opens for the commit, fill in a title and comment for the change.

10. Select whether to make the change directly to the main branch or to create a new branch for testing the change.

If the changes were made to the main branch, then the workflow should now fire with the updated settings. If a new branch was created, then a pull request is needed to test the changes; see Chapter 12 for more information on pull requests.

Index

A

© Stacy Cashmore 2022
S. Cashmore, *Beginning Azure Static Web Apps*, https://doi.org/10.1007/978-1-4842-8146-8

Printed in the United States
by Baker & Taylor Publisher Services